Fort Worth is cooking!

by
RENIE STEVES

Nutritionist
GEORGIA KOSTAS, MPH, RD, LD
The Cooper Clinic

Foreword by
DEBORAH MONCRIEF

CUISINE
CONCEPTS
Publisher

FORT WORTH IS COOKING!

Copyright © 1993 by Renie Steves

All rights reserved. No portion of this book may be reproduced without written permission from the author.

Printed in the United States of America

ISBN 0-9635470-1-1

Library of Congress Cataloging-In-Publication data

Cuisine Concepts

All recipes are printed with permission of authors.
Photographs printed with permission of Mark V. Davis.
Nutritional information printed with permission of Georgia Kostas.

SPECIAL THANKS TO

Alicia Bradshaw, Jason Wills, Editorial Assistants
Mark V. Davis, Photography
Sterling W. Steves, Wine & History Consultant
Bill Bostelmann, Flowers on the Square
LeWay Composing Service, Inc., Design and Layout
Sprint Press, Printing
Jayroe Litho, Lithography
Jill Fortney, Personal Image Consultant
Neiman Marcus
The Worthington Hotel
Fort Worth Star-Telegram
Jane Larimore, American Paint Horse Champions
Jerome Stock, Cowtown Corrals, Saddle Horses
Wendy Davis, Tarantula Corporation
La Dean, Glassware
Maverick Fine Western Wear
Texas College of Osteopathic Medicine
Fort Worth Park & Recreation Department

FOREWORD *by Deborah Moncrief*

Deborah Moncrief, patron saint of Fort Worth arts and history and lifelong advocate of Cowtown culture, has a profound interest in food and wine.

Good food and fond memories mix like ingredients in an exquisitely crafted soufflé. What wonderful recollections I have of food and fun growing up in Tarrant County.

I can remember rancher E.D. Farmer hosting a picnic for local friends each June at the Mary's Creek picnic grounds, which then was a part of his ranch. Everyone looked forward to the incomparable beef from his herd and the fresh vegetables from his sprawling ranch garden. The men dug deep pits and cooked steaks, ribs and briskets over wood fires. Women in the area prepared all of the trimmings. Dessert was homemade ice cream churned on the spot.

The change of seasons from autumn to winter takes me back to a special rite of fall. I will always associate the first Norther cold front with hog-killing time. As many as 20 neighbors would gather with the family at the ranch house for the day. When the work was done, and the last ham hung in the smokehouse, we feasted on grand Texas-size meals. Pork chops and cracklings, cooked on the wood stove in the kitchen, were accompanied by zesty black-eyed peas, corn on the cob, and hot homemade country biscuits dripping with sorghum syrup. We would cook fresh pork sausage and everyone would sample the seasoning. Then we'd pack it into long cloth tubes and send everybody home with a helping.

The tantalizing aroma of home-baked bread from the original Mrs. Baird is still etched in my memory. Mrs. Baird's horse-drawn bread wagon delivered warm, crusty loaves to my grandmother, Mrs. George Beggs, each day. The wagon stopped at all of the great houses along Summit Avenue, dispensing delicious bread to the cooks.

In the early 1900s, lunch was the most important meal of the day. Men would leave their offices and come home for hearty noontime dinners with their families, and rest during the hottest part of the day.

Back then, a restaurant lunch was quite an event. The lovely King's Tea Room in downtown was a special treat for lunch or afternoon tea. Chicken á la King was the favored meal of the day. The Pink Rooster Tea Room in Stripling's Department Store was famous for homemade chili with saltine crackers, while Monnig's Tea Room specialized in hot roast beef sandwiches. Pangburn's Soda Fountain and Candy Shop had long counters lined with jar after jar of beautiful candy. One could enjoy a sandwich or salad for lunch, then delight the palate with ice cream sodas, chocolate sundaes, fountain Coca-Cola or limeade. Pangburn's was next to The Fair, an elegant department store. Its owner, Lionel Bevan, often would

bring his family into Pangburn's and visit with the other customers.

The Siebold Steak House was tremendously popular for lunch, especially with the men. The steaks were enormous. I also recall the delicious barbecue sandwiches at Turner & Dingee grocery store in downtown. People would go in and shop for groceries, and take the sandwiches home, or call for delivery.

The Mexican Inn was not far away. I loved the Mexican plate, which had a taco, enchilada, rice and beans. Its owner, Tiffin Hall, lived nearby in the Blackstone Hotel and bragged that he had made his fortune in two blocks of downtown Fort Worth.

Tamales were sold from a cart on Seventh Street near the Trinity River viaduct. The owner, complete with handlebar mustache, would open the cart and steam would billow all around with the spicy scent of tamales. I would drive there after school with my friends, buy a dozen tamales, and eat them in the nearby park.

As residential neighborhoods developed on the west bank of the river, West Seventh Street and Camp Bowie became major business thoroughfares. We bought tangy chili dogs at the Coney Island hot dog stand before or after a movie at the Hollywood, Worth or Majestic theaters on Seventh Street, which was known as "Show

Row." The Triple X Root Beer stand nearby was said to serve the best hamburger in town. Who could forget Steve Murrin's fabulous ham sandwiches, with a bowl of beans on the side, at his Camp Bowie restaurant? We would stop at Steve's on our way to the ranch and pick up our order at the counter. If there was a sandwich hall of fame, Steve would have been among the first inducted. Lucile's now occupies that building.

The North Side has always retained the flavor of the Wild West. After the rodeo people frequented Theo's Restaurant, where some would eat mountain oysters. In the summertime, watermelon gardens sprang up in vacant lots around town. Enterprising folks would put huge coolers full of icy cold watermelon for sale in the lot during the sweltering dog days of summer. Fuqua's and Carshon's delicatessens introduced Northern flavors to Fort Worth.

While dining out in the evening was rare in those days, members of society would socialize in private clubs. For an evening out, the Fort Worth Club was unmatched. Everyone went there. Most of the club was reserved exclusively for its gentlemen members, but ladies were welcome in the 12th floor's formal dining room. The hot water cornbread served with each meal is forever enshrined in my memory.

And let's not forget the Texas Club, owned by Boston Smith. I am told that the food there was fabulous. Unfortunately, I was too young to go and never experienced it firsthand.

There has been and always will be great pleasure and reward in the rapport between companionship and good food. They seem always to accompany one another in my fondest memories. This is why we are so fortunate to have Renie Steves in Fort Worth, bringing her special touch and talents to enhance our appreciation of both. I know you will enjoy "Fort Worth Is Cooking!" Our Fort Worth culinary heritage lives on in these fine restaurants.

See you in Cowtown.

Deborah Mancini

OVERVIEW OF TARRANT COUNTY HISTORY *by Sterling W. Steves*

Fort Worth was founded near the Trinity River where the courthouse stands today. The founding was occasioned by the arrival on June 6, 1846, of Major Ripley Arnold and a company of the Second Dragoons. Arnold elected to camp on a bluff which looks north over the confluence of two branches of the river. The bluff was a natural place to build a fort; its high ground was essential for military purposes. The new fort was named for General William Jennings Worth, Arnold's commander, who died of cholera in San Antonio two days before the Dragoons arrived in Tarrant County.

Fort Worth was established to protect settlers in the area from marauding Indians. The fort became a hub for traders and a magnet for those who served the soldiers' needs, and others who came for shelter.

The fort was challenged only once. A band of Indians came to the fort because they were being chased by several hundred Comanche Indians. The fort had only 42 troops at the time. Major Arnold refused to let the Comanches enter. To scare them away, the soldiers fired a six-pound howitzer cannon. It belched forth and dropped a shell in the Comanches' midst, and frightened them sufficiently that they were satisfied to take three head of cattle and leave.

The county grew in the years prior to the Civil War, and reached a population of approximately 6,000 people. A dispute arose over the establishment of the county seat (this was common in Texas). Birdville, now part of Haltom City, was the original location. Envious of Birdville's distinction, Fort Worth staged a fraudulent election in November of 1856, and the seat was moved.

In 1866, the new Chisholm Trail passed near Fort Worth, bringing enormous herds of cattle up from South Texas and on to Wichita, Kansas. Fort Worth became a very popular stop along the trail. Cowboys would come off the dusty trail and ride into town to bathe, eat, play cards, drink whiskey, chase ladies of the evening and generally raise hell. Once the town marshal's office reported that there were only 298 fights; it was a slow night. An area rife with bars, saloons, brothels and gambling joints sprang up south of the fort along what was then known as Rusk Street. The neighborhood earned the nickname "Hell's Half Acre" for its dens of iniquity. The cowboys would spend a rowdy night in town, and then go back on the trail, herding their cattle north.

Hell's Half Acre, where the Tarrant County Convention Center now stands, remained as such for decades and was really not dismantled until the

6

convention center was built. The main street, Rusk Street, was named after a signer of the Texas Declaration of Independence and veteran of the Battle of San Jacinto. The area was so bad that Rusk Street was renamed Commerce Street because local people thought Rusk was too good a name for such a rough part of town.

West Texas was settled with the aid of three things, according to Professor Walter Prescott Webb, a noted historian at the University of Texas. They were the windmill, the six-shooter, and barbed wire. The windmill was necessary for water; the six-shooter defended against personal attack; and barbed wire kept cattle from wandering afar. Barbed wire led to many range wars between settlers and cattle interests who had enjoyed years of free-range grazing for their herds.

Fort Worth was incorporated as a town in 1873. It continued to grow with people migrating from the overcrowded cities in the East to search for land and independence in the wide-open West. Many of the great cattlemen with huge ranches west of Fort Worth built beautiful mansions here and moved their families into town. The ladies could shop, raise children, and avoid suffering the indignities and hardships of ranch living. Many of the cattle barons' homes were built along Penn Street and Summit Avenue. Thistle Hill, constructed in

1903 as a wedding gift from W.T. Waggoner to his daughter Electra Waggoner Wharton, is a glorious example of the great homes the wealthy ranchers built.

In 1876 the Texas & Pacific railroad came to Fort Worth, and the city became a boom town. By 1902 the Chisholm Trail ended on Fort Worth's North Side, where cattle were driven into the stockyards and sold to packing houses such as Swift and Armour. The beef was processed here and shipped North in refrigerated rail cars. Fort Worth became a major point of distribution, and remains an important railroad city today. The city was a packing and processing center until the 1950s when the plants were closed. Changes in the beef industry drove cattle feed lot operations to different parts of the country.

In early 1911, oil was discovered in the Ranger Field west of town. With this rich find, more people poured into Fort Worth seeking their fortune. At one point, martial law was declared in the Ranger Field to stop thefts of oil, leases, and equipment. Fort Worth was a major oil industry business hub until after World War II. Thereafter the major companies moved to Houston.

In World War I, Camp Bowie was built on the West Side. There, 100,000 troops were trained by the 36th Infantry Division for duty in France. The camp was closed after the war. That area developed rapidly into the neighborhood we know as Arlington Heights.

At the beginning of World War II, Consolidated Vultee built a large aircraft plant in Fort Worth. The plant produced the B-24 Liberator, a four-engine bomber that flew in the European theater. The city drew more aircraft manufacturers in later years. Bell Helicopter came to Hurst, and Chance Vought came to Grand Prairie, bringing support industries along with them. With the development of Dallas/Fort Worth International Airport and construction of the new Alliance Industrial Airport, Tarrant County has a firm stake in international air travel and cargo operations.

Tarrant County residents have been committed to cultural affairs for generations. Fort Worth has the oldest opera company in Texas. The symphony and ballet are renowned. The Van Cliburn competition confirms that Fort Worth has been a 'piano town' since Major Arnold's wife brought hers here in 1850. The Kimbell and Amon Carter Museums, and the Museum of Modern Art reflect our passion for art. Top quality medical and educational institutions abound in our cities. The philanthropy and charity of residents has been substantial over the years. The most noted charitable event is the Jewel Ball. Since its inception in 1954, it has raised more than $9 million for Cook-Fort Worth Children's Medical Center, including $1 million annually in the last four years.

Over its colorful, 150-year history Tarrant County has grown to approximately 1.2 million people. Who would have envisioned this when Major Arnold Ripley rode his horse up the bluff over the Trinity and said, "This is where we will camp."

Sterling W. Steves is a board-certified civil trial lawyer and wine columnist whose love of food, wine and his wife makes it easier to bear hunger pangs from missed meals when she is working.

TABLE OF CONTENTS

 Wine Suggestions   Recipe Modifications

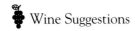 Wine Suggestions   Recipe Modifications

INTRODUCTION *by Renie Steves*

*Renie Steves, CEO of Cuisine Concepts,
is a dedicated cooking instructor, wine educator,
food stylist, and consultant.*

From stockyards to skyscrapers, medicine to museums, railroads to runways, lakes to links, hospitals to horse shows, and universities to the zoo, Tarrant County's diversity draws together people from all walks of life. And they all like to eat. This book will introduce you to the favorite chefs and restaurateurs, and to cuisine as interesting as the people who create it.

Wherever you go, the chef can be readily identified.

Cooking is the only profession with a universal uniform of a crisply starched white jacket, tall hat and checkered pants. This is good, because our varied group of local restaurateurs and chefs could answer roll-call at the United Nations. Enjoy the sumptuous dishes they offer, while relishing the personality and charisma of each restaurant and the men and women behind it.

There is a lot to be said for Tarrant County. Downtown Fort Worth's Sundance Square bustles with activity. Wide-open spaces abound in the cultural district, and boots, silver belt buckles and cowboy hats are as common there as they are in the Stockyards on the North Side. Arlington boasts the Texas Rangers, and its new stadium will be among the best in major league baseball. In Northeast Tarrant County, a hot spot of 21st century development, beautiful homes mingle with pasture land.

With the help of my protégés in Cuisine Concepts and The French Apron cooking schools, we have explored new foods and ingredients as well as old favorites. Over the last 15 years we have progressed from ordering red peppers via overnight delivery from Houston, to buying fennel, prosciutto and fresh mozzarella from local merchants.

Cooking schools are increasing the awareness of

unique foods, improving people's ability to understand menus, and influencing the fresh approaches that many local chefs have taken. Our residents have embraced new cuisines, and grocers are working with us to accommodate the supply needs for new tastes and new flavors. For unusual flavors found in these recipes, check Pendery's Mexican Chile Supply, George's Grocery, Koko's Grocery and Take Stock frozen stocks at the market.

The creation of this book has been aided by several very special people. My wonderful husband of 35 years, Sterling Steves, continues to support my publishing projects. He wrote the charming Overview of Tarrant County History which begins on page 10. Deborah Moncrief generously shared her recollections of Tarrant County with us in the Foreword. Georgia Kostas of the Cooper Clinic contributed nutrition knowledge and expertise, and added depth and timeliness to this book.

My keen-eyed friend, Tony Furfari, proofread hundreds of pages of copy. Keith Crow restored our computer hardware and data after an untimely lightening strike. Carol Bradshaw, my fitness trainer, contributed bursts of creativity to the essays. Spencer and Linda Wertz and Bryant Griffith harvested flowers at dawn for a photo shoot. Photographer Mark Davis and my energetic staff,

Alicia Bradshaw, Jason Wills, and DeAnna Koch, have taken this book beyond the standard of excellence set in my first book, "Dallas Is Cooking!" My deepest thanks to these wonderful friends.

I am especially grateful to Antinori Wines of Tuscany, Piper-Sonoma Sparkling Wines, Fall Creek Vineyards, and others who allowed us to use their wines in photography and promotion. Our civic and business leaders have been very supportive, and I thank them very much.

The grape cluster at the end of most recipes suggests complementary wines. The wheat sheave offers healthful recipe modifications, while Lighter Bites following each essay recommend lower fat menu choices.

This book is for you — to prepare favorites at home, to guide exploration of our restaurants, and to share Tarrant County style with faraway friends and visitors. Welcome to the wild, wonderful west! Happy dining — in or out!

TUNA ALLA GRAPPA

OSTRICH 3G

LINGUINE CARBONARA

PAPPARDELLE ALLO STRUZZO

PROSCIUTTO E MELONE

MASCARPONE
with Raspberry Sauce

Ciao! Has the chef escaped from the kitchen on this busy night? Carlo Crocci often is the first person one sees at Bella West. With sparkling eyes and a ready wit, Crocci dashes from table to kitchen, greeting patrons by name along the way.

The energetic restaurateur was born in Tuscany, and worked with chefs in Spain and Italy before coming to the United States. Crocci thrives on paying attention to every detail of his business. He cooks, collects wine, raises the herbs and flowers which grace plates and tables, and plans and executes the daily specials.

"In Italy people eat a lot of game," says Crocci. Ostrich, with its juicy red meat, is a favorite among the specials. Patrons also enjoy the mild but tasteful buffalo tartare served with toast, onions, lemon and olive paste. Crocci butchers all of the meat, cutting everything to order. The thick veal chop or succulent sushi-grade tuna steak, both deglazed with a pungent Italian brandy called grappa, have five-star looks and taste.

The house salad is packed with romaine, mushrooms, black olives, pickled peppers, tomatoes, and Parmesan. Different vegetable side dishes, from polenta to broccoli to layered potatoes, please the palate. Crocci's motto is "generous portions that are delicious and unique."

Order a vino from the fine Italian wine list to accompany your meal, or choose one of a generous selection of wines by the glass. Many of the wines are not available elsewhere. Crocci says, "For the value, Italian wine is better than any other."

Bella West offers al fresco dining on its pleasant patio with lush plants and fans that stir gentle breezes. Crocci dines here in his private sanctuary after the last guest is served. As a special concession to his patrons, the restaurant carries De Cecco pastas, cheeses such as Italian Parmigiano-Reggiano, gorgonzola, mascarpone and mozzarella, genuine prosciutto, and other delicacies.

LIGHTER BITES

Select your meal from among the Funghi Paseano (with less oil), minestrone soup, the Insalata Della Casa with dressing on the side, Pollo alla Cacciatora or Scalloppine al Marsala, and Frutta Fresca di Stagione.

*5139 Camp Bowie Blvd.
Fort Worth, TX 76107
817/738-1700*

TUNA ALLA GRAPPA

Tuna is similar to steak in texture and becomes dry and stringy if overcooked. Grappa is a clear type of brandy made from the skins and stems of the grapes.

> 2 10-ounce fresh tuna steaks
>   Salt and pepper
> 1 clove garlic, minced
> 2 tablespoons olive oil
> 1/4 cup grappa
>   Juice of 1/2 lemon
>   Fresh chopped parsley

Season the tuna steaks with salt, pepper and garlic on both sides. Heat olive oil in a heavy skillet until lightly smoking. Add tuna steaks and cook to rare or medium rare, turning once. Add grappa and flame quickly. Add lemon juice and parsley and serve immediately. *Serves 2.*

 Tuna and all fish are heart-healthy foods. This recipe may be prepared with two 6-ounce tuna steaks and 2 teaspoons of olive oil to reduce fat.

 Pio Cesare Arneis (Italian White)
Michele Chiarlo Barbera d'Asti (Italian Red)

OSTRICH 3G

Ostrich is a juicy red meat, so beef and veal stock are good substitutes for ostrich stock.

> 2 4-ounce ostrich filets*
>   Salt and pepper
> 1 clove garlic
> 2 tablespoons butter
> 1/4 cup grappa
> 1/2 cup sliced mushrooms
> 1/4 cup ostrich stock
>   (or veal Take Stock)
> 1/4 cup grated mozzarella cheese

Pound the ostrich filets lightly with a mallet, and remove any stringy parts. Season the meat on both sides with salt, pepper and garlic. Melt butter in a heavy sauté pan and add the meat. Sauté ostrich filets on each side, add grappa and flame. Remove the meat to a platter and keep warm. Add mushrooms to the sauce remaining in pan. Add stock and reduce by half. Add mozzarella to sauce and stir to incorporate into sauce. Pour sauce over meat and serve immediately. *Serves 2.*

* Ostrich is available through Breezy Hill Meat Company in Bowie, Texas.

 Use 2 teaspoons olive oil in place of the butter, and the fat in this recipe is reduced by half.

 Corvo-Duca Enrico (Italian Red)
Gaja Barolo (Italian Red)

LINGUINE CARBONARA

De Cecco, an excellent brand of dried pasta, is available at the restaurant, George's Grocery or Roy Pope Grocery.

    1 pound linguine
    2 tablespoons olive oil
  1/4 cup chopped onion
    4 ounces apple-smoked bacon
  1/2 cup sliced mushrooms
    2 cloves garlic, minced
    2 cups heavy cream
  1/4 cup grated
      Parmigiano-Reggiano cheese
      Salt and pepper

Cook the pasta in plenty of boiling water until al dente. Heat the olive oil in a large skillet. Sauté the onions, bacon, mushrooms and garlic. Drain the cooked pasta and add to the skillet mixture. Add cream and cheese, and taste for salt and pepper. *Serves 4.*

 This dish is rich in vitamin A and all vitamin Bs. To lower the fat and cholesterol, use 4 ounces of Canadian bacon, 2 cups evaporated skim milk, and no-stick cooking spray with just 2 teaspoons olive oil.

 Frescobaldi Pomino Il Benefizio (Italian White)
Castellare Chianti Classico (Italian Red)

PAPPARDELLE ALLO STRUZZO

Pappardelle is a 1-inch wide noodle. The recipe is best when made with ostrich or buffalo, but ground veal may be substituted.

    2 tablespoons olive oil
  1/4 cup chopped onion
    1 large clove garlic
    8 ounces ground ostrich meat*
  1/2 cup tomato paste
  1/2 cup red wine
  1/2 cup ostrich stock (or Take Stock)
    4 ounces gorgonzola cheese
      Dash red pepper
   14 ounces pappardelle pasta
  1/4 cup grated
      Parmigiano-Reggiano cheese

To make the sauce, heat olive oil in a large saucepan and sauté onions, garlic and meat. Add tomato paste, red wine and stock. Cook for approximately 20 to 30 minutes. Add gorgonzola, salt and red pepper to taste.

Cook the pasta in a large pot of boiling water according to package directions. Drain and serve with sauce and grated cheese. *Serves 4.*

 Ostrich is very lean. Use 2 ounces cheese and 2 teaspoons olive oil. Red, yellow or green onions, which contain anti-oxidants, may be substituted to protect against heart disease and cancer.

 Prunotto Barbera d'Alba (Italian Red)
Banfi Brunello Di Montalcino (Italian Red)

PROSCIUTTO E MELONE

Authentic Italian Prosciutto di Parma is available at Bella Italia West.

>   6 slices melon
>   6 slices prosciutto di Parma
> 1/4 cup grated Parmigiano-Reggiano
>   Fresh herbs or parsley, for garnish

Select a ripe, medium-sized melon. Cut melon into slices and remove seeds and rind. Wrap each slice with prosciutto and arrange the melon slices on a platter. Add shavings of Parmigiano-Reggiano. Garnish with a touch of fresh herbs or parsley and serve. *Serves 2.*

 Lungarotti Torre di Giano (Italian White)
Antinori Orvieto (Italian White)

MASCARPONE *with Raspberry Sauce*

Mascarpone is somewhat similar to American cream cheese.

>   2 tablespoons granulated sugar
>   2 cups raspberries, fresh or frozen
> 1/4 cup grappa
>   2 cups mascarpone cheese
>   Fresh raspberries, for garnish
>   Mint leaves, for garnish

Heat sugar in a heavy skillet until it caramelizes and turns golden brown. Add raspberries and cook down slightly. Strain sauce through a sieve, pressing hard to extract all the juice. Return sauce to skillet and flame with grappa. Pour over mascarpone. Garnish with fresh berries and mint leaves. *Serves 4.*

 Vietti Grappa (Italian Brandy)

BISTRO BAGATELLE

BAVAROIS OF SALMON
with Chive Beurre Blanc

SALADE DES CHAMPS AUX POMMES DE TERRE DOUCES

CHOCOLATE MARQUISE

LE BLANC DE POULET MARINE AU PISTOU

At first glance, the cottage in downtown Arlington appears as inconspicuous as its name. Bistro Bagatelle, French for "a trifle," is a delightful surprise. Husband-and-wife team Gerard and Marcelle Bahon welcome patrons into Bagatelle's homelike setting. The cozy, refined atmosphere is attributable to its location, a home built in 1939.

Appetites are quickly appeased as guests settle in one of four small sunlit rooms. Waiters whisk a complimentary Tapenade hors d'oeuvre to the table while diners peruse the menu. Bagatelle's wine list displays the labels of wines, ranging from the usual Clos Du Bois Chardonnay to a rare Jaboulet-Vercherre Chassagne-Montrachet.

Bistro Bagatelle

Bahon says people are returning to "everyday" food. One of the French bistro's signature dishes, Bavarois of Salmon, is a strikingly beautiful example of Bahon's innovative "everyday" creations. Artfully molded salmon slices are filled with crisp field greens, and surrounded with a butter sauce. A meal of three grilled fishes — tuna, salmon and swordfish — centered with a mountain of pasta in a pool of demi-glace sauce, and a White Bean Cassoulet of Lamb are among the other delicacies. The feast can continue with an Apple Tart with Honey Cinnamon Ice Cream and Caramel Sauce, and an abundant offering of cordials and cognacs.

Bahon came to America in 1970 from the jagged coast of the Brittany region of France. He worked with mentor chef Andre René in New York, and served as executive chef for Dallas' Grand Kempinski, Fairmont and Adolphus hotels. His move in May 1990 to Arlington did not go unnoticed. Bistro Bagatelle has been featured in Food and Wine Magazine's "50 under $50" and received the "Best of the Best Award" from the Award Academy of the Restaurant Industry.

Even with that under his belt, Bahon says "you cannot take yourself too seriously." As a chef, he describes himself as demanding. "I like to think I'm generous," he says, "but people must prove themselves." Bistro Bagatelle is the culmination of Bahon's talent and experience — and hardly a trifle.

LIGHTER BITES

Order Raviole of Snails and Eggplant, any salad with dressing on the side, any of the entrees (except duck or linguine), and share a dessert.

406 West Abram
Arlington, TX 76010
817/261-0488

BAVAROIS OF SALMON *with Chive Beurre Blanc*

The salad should be cool and crisp, and the salmon slightly rare. Serve it quickly so the greens are not wilted by the warm salmon.

CHIVE BEURRE BLANC
    3 **shallots, minced**
    1 **teaspoon crushed white peppercorns**
    1 **bay leaf**
    1 **cup dry white wine**
  1/2 **cup heavy cream**
2 1/2 **sticks unsalted butter**
       Salt and pepper
       Juice of 1 lemon
    2 **tablespoons minced fresh chives**

BAVAROIS OF SALMON
   18 **ounces Norwegian salmon fillets, sliced very thin**
   11 **tablespoons unsalted butter, room temperature**
       Salt and pepper
    6 **cups mixed greens (Boston, red leaf, radicchio, Belgian endive, arugula, mizuna)**
       Vinaigrette dressing
    1 **tomato, peeled, seeded and diced**

Place the shallots, crushed pepper, bay leaf and wine in a small saucepan, and reduce until all the liquid has evaporated. Add cream and cool slowly to thicken. Whisk in the butter (a tablespoon at a time) over low heat, until incorporated. Do not allow the mixture to boil. Season with salt and pepper, and add lemon juice to taste. Strain through a fine sieve or china cap. Keep warm in a water bath or thermos (never too hot, the sauce might separate). Add chives just before serving.

To prepare the salmon, coat six 6-ounce soufflé dishes generously with softened butter so the salmon will not stick to the dish. Layer slices of salmon, covering the bottom of the dish and rising up the edges, until each dish is completely covered. Season with salt and pepper and cover with plastic wrap. Repeat with remaining soufflé dishes. Steam salmon for 2 to 3 minutes. Remove the plastic wrap and drain any liquid which may accumulate in the dish. With a small knife, carefully loosen the salmon from the edge of the dish.

Tear the mixed greens into pieces and toss with a small amount of your favorite vinaigrette dressing. Pack the steamed salmon-lined soufflé dishes with seasoned greens. Cover with a plate and quickly flip over. Tap the dish to unmold the salmon. Quickly serve with a touch of chive sauce around the salmon and garnish with tomato. *Serves 6.*

Note: If you do not have a steamer, you could build one with a deep pot, a colander, boiling water and an airtight lid. It might take a little longer to cook but it will work fine.

 Prepare with half-and half, and just 1 stick of margarine. Use Pam on dish.

 Adler Fels Fumé Blanc (California White)
Duboeuf Grenache (French Rosé)

SALADE DES CHAMPS AUX POMMES DE TERRE DOUCES
(Field Salad With Sweet Potato Slices)

Safflower, olive or walnut oil may be used.

- 6 **ounces field salad greens (lamb's lettuce, arugula, mizuna, red oak)**
- 1 **head radicchio (3 leaves per person)**
- 1 **large sweet potato**
- 1 **tablespoon oil for sautéeing potato**
- 1 **cup grapeseed oil**
- 2 **tablespoons lemon juice**
  Salt and pepper
- 3/4 **cup chopped pecans**

Wash lettuces and radicchio and arrange artistically on salad plates. Peel sweet potato and cut into very thin, even round slices. Sauté sweet potato slices over high heat for about 15 seconds. Arrange on top of the salad leaves.

Mix grapeseed oil and lemon juice. Add salt and pepper to taste. Ladle over salad and sprinkle with chopped pecans. *Serves 4.*

 Brush sweet potatoes with 1 teaspoon butter and broil 1 to 2 minutes per side. Omit pecans and use only 1/2 cup oil or substitute no-oil or low-fat dressing.

 Pine Ridge Chenin Blanc (California White)
Hugel Riesling (French White)

CHOCOLATE MARQUISE

Berry puree, confectioners' sugar and mint garnish add color to this cool, creamy dish.

- 2 **ounces sweet dark chocolate**
- 1 **vanilla bean**
- 2 **tablespoons espresso**
- 2 **egg yolks**
- 1 1/2 **cups heavy cream**
- 1 1/2 **sticks unsalted butter**
- 1 1/2 **cups cocoa**
- 2 **tablespoons water**
- 1/2 **cup granulated sugar**
- 1/4 **cup egg white**

Melt chocolate with vanilla bean, and add espresso. Whip egg yolk over barely simmering water, until a ribbon is formed. Whip heavy cream and set aside. Blend butter and cocoa, and add chocolate mixture and yolks. Cook water and sugar to about 260 degrees. Whip whites and drizzle in sugar syrup. Fold meringue and whipped cream into egg mixture and put in 8x4x3-inch terrine. Refrigerate overnight. Serves 10.

 Taittinger Brut (French Champagne)
Piper Sonoma Blanc de Noir (California Sparkling Wine)

LE BLANC DE POULET MARINE AU PISTOU
(Chilled Marinated Chicken Breast With Green Sauce)

This is a great choice for a backyard party. It can be prepared in advance.

> 4 boneless, skinless chicken breasts
> 2 tablespoons clarified butter
> 1/2 pound fresh tomatoes
> 1/2 bunch basil, divided use
> 2 cloves garlic
> 1 bunch watercress
> 1/3 cup olive oil
> 1/2 cup half-and-half
> Salt and pepper

To prepare the chicken breasts, first season with salt and pepper. Place the chicken in a non-stick pan with clarified butter and cook over very low heat for 6 minutes. Pat chicken dry.

Peel, seed, and cut the tomatoes into cubes. Cut 8 basil leaves into julienne and mix with the diced tomatoes. Add salt and pepper.

For the pistou (green sauce), clean the cloves of garlic and pick watercress leaves from the stems. Dip the leaves of watercress for one second in the boiling water and place immediately on ice. Put the remaining basil leaves, the watercress, and garlic in a blender. While blending, add olive oil slowly. Add the half-and-half to the blender. Add salt and pepper to taste. Keep chilled.

Cut the breast of chicken diagonally into 3 or 4 slices. Place on dinner plates. Top each chicken breast with tomatoes. Pour green sauce around the chicken. Keep chilled. *Serves 4.*

 Tomatoes and watercress add lots of vitamins A and C. To reduce fat, use just 1 tablespoon margarine, 1/8 cup oil, and 1/4 cup half-and-half.

 Kendall-Jackson Sauvignon Blanc (California White)
Beringer Gamay Beaujolais (California Red)

CHILLED CANTALOUPE SOUP
with Honey & Lime

WILD RICE CAKES

ROASTED LOIN OF LAMB
with Garlic, Thyme and Sherry Vinegar Jus

SAFFRON SORBET

BROILED SEA SCALLOPS
with a Juice of Vegetables 'a la Grecque' and Virgin Olive Oil

Seven years ago, Cacharel was one of Arlington's best kept secrets, hidden high on the ninth floor of the Brookhollow Two Building. Today, stellar quality has elevated the restaurant among the Metroplex's vanguard establishments.

The dynamic duo behind the scene is Jean-Claude Adam and Chef Hans Bergmann, who know no boundaries to hospitality. The wait staff's impeccable service subtly spoils guests. "Hans is a natural with food," Adam says. "He has vision. He cooks, and it works." Bergmann is always willing to accommodate a special request.

Located in lovely north Arlington, Cacharel is a perfect rendezvous for business and pleasure. The restaurant offers a stunning panoramic view of the city. Its private reception room, which accommodates 100 guests, is a wonderful place for corporate dinners and wedding events. A full-time wedding consultant is available to coordinate such events.

Many a lifetime commitment has been made with Cacharel as the backdrop. Bergmann recalls one gentleman slipping an engagement ring into his prospective fiancée's champagne glass to surprise her. He succeeded — she almost swallowed it.

Adam and Bergmann are attempting to soften the formal image of the restaurant. "People are looking for casual dining," Bergmann says. "They don't want to dress up. A coat and tie are not required. We're trying to get away from being a special-occasion restaurant."

Bergmann cites French Chef Roger Vergé as his hero, for his open-minded attitude and Provençal cuisine. That influence may be seen in his Fillet of John Dory on a bed of Honey Glazed Onions with a Fresh Tomato Sauce infused with Basil. Cacharel's signature menu is Sautéed Snails served in a Cream Sauce with Jicama, Ancho Peppers, Anaheim Peppers, Garlic and Lime, and Roasted Breast of Duck on a Cassis Sauce. To accentuate the meal, the wine list offers a well-rounded mix of California and French selections. Crown the evening with Phyllo Layers filled with "White Chocolate" Mousse and Garnished with Fresh Raspberries — a rich end to a memorable experience at Cacharel.

LIGHTER BITES

Choose Salad With Warm Mussels and Sea Scallops, Fillet of Farm-Raised Sturgeon With Sautéed Shrimp, and Poached Red Wine Apples with Cinnamon Sauce (omit ice cream). Ask for dressings and sauces on the side.

Brookhollow Two
2221 East Lamar Blvd.
Arlington, TX 76006
817/640-9981

21

CHILLED CANTALOUPE SOUP *with Honey & Lime*

If lavender honey is unavailable, substitute high-quality plain honey.

> 2 cantaloupes
> 2 tablespoons lavender honey
> Juice of 2 limes
> 8 fresh mint sprigs (divided use)

Halve cantaloupes and scoop out seeds. Scoop 20 melon balls and set aside for garnish. Cut remaining melon into chunks and puree in blender until smooth. In a small pan, cook honey until it foams and caramelizes. Lower heat and add lime juice. Stir to deglaze the pan and let cool.

Julienne 4 mint sprigs. Stir together with puree and honey mixture, and refrigerate for several hours. To serve, ladle soup into chilled bowls. Garnish with melon balls and mint sprig. *Serves 4.*

 This healthy soup is a great idea for brunch or dessert. It is refreshing and high in vitamins A and C.

 La Vielle Ferme Cotes du Luberon (French White)
Meridian Chardonnay (California White)

WILD RICE CAKES

These savory cakes are baked, rather than sautéed or fried.

> 3/4 cup cooked wild rice
> 1/2 cup finely diced red and
>   yellow bell pepper
> 1/2 cup finely diced zucchini
>   Pinch of arrowroot
>   Salt and pepper
> 2 egg whites, beaten until stiff
> 1 1/2 teaspoons olive oil

Place wild rice, bell pepper, zucchini, and arrowroot in a mixing bowl, and season with salt and pepper. Fold in egg whites. Spoon small cakes onto greased pan and bake at 375 degrees until golden brown. *Serves 6.*

 Go for color. Red and yellow bell pepper are very healthy and contain vitamins A and C.

 Chalk Hill Chardonnay (California White)
Reserve St Martin Mourvèdre (French Red)

ROAST LOIN OF LAMB *with Garlic, Thyme and Sherry Vinegar Jus*

Deglazing, heating liquid in a pan and stirring to incorporate, can be done on top of the stove.

- 2 8-ounce lamb loins, trimmed
  Salt and pepper
- 1 tablespoon olive oil
- 8 garlic cloves, peeled
- 10 sprigs fresh thyme
- 2 tablespoons sherry vinegar
- 1 tomato, peeled and diced
- 1 cup lamb or veal stock
  Cayenne pepper
  Fresh thyme, for garnish

Sprinkle lamb with salt and pepper and sear over high heat in olive oil. Add garlic cloves and thyme. Place pan in preheated 400-degree oven and cook to medium rare, about 3 to 4 minutes. Wrap loins in foil, and set aside to rest for 10 minutes before slicing. Heat pan in oven and deglaze with sherry vinegar. Add diced tomato and cook until vinegar evaporates. Add stock and bake 3 minutes. Add drippings from lamb. Season to taste.

Remove garlic cloves and keep warm. Strain sauce and spoon onto hot plates. Slice lamb and arrange over sauce, garnishing with garlic cloves and a sprig of thyme. *Serves 4.*

 Sear lamb with just 1/2 tablespoon olive oil.

 Gruaud-Larose St. Julien (French Red)
Caymus Cabernet Sauvignon (California Red)

SAFFRON SORBET

The flavor of this unusual sorbet comes from the stigmas of a small crocus.

- 1/3 cup sugar plus 2 tablespoons
- 1/4 cup water
  Pinch of saffron
- 1 cup freshly squeezed orange juice
- 1 tablespoon Pernod
- 1/4 cup white wine
- 2 tablespoons vodka

Place sugar and water in a saucepan and cook over medium-high heat, stirring to dissolve sugar. Continue to cook until syrup reaches a boil. Add saffron and boil for 2 minutes. Allow mixture to cool and mix in remaining ingredients. Freeze in a sorbet or ice cream machine. Pipe into glasses and serve. *Serves 6.*

 Piper-Heidsieck Extra Dry (French Champagne)
Schramsberg Blanc de Blanc (California Sparkling Wine)

BROILED SEA SCALLOPS
with a Puree of Vegetables 'A La Grecque' and Virgin Olive Oil

"A la Grecque" is a technique of cooking vegetables with parsley, celery, thyme, bay leaf, coriander, fennel, peppercorns, lemon juice and olive oil, and serving them very cold.

  1 **pound tomatoes, peeled and seeded**
1 1/4 **pounds fennel, cut julienne**
 10 **whole peppercorns**
 30 **whole coriander seeds**
  2 **cups white wine**
  2 **cups water**
  1 **cup extra-virgin olive oil,**
     plus 2 tablespoons
  4 **baby eggplant**
     Salt and pepper
 20 **giant sea scallops**
     Cilantro leaves, for garnish

Puree tomatoes in blender, and bring to boil in a saucepan. Add fennel, peppercorns, coriander, white wine and water. Simmer uncovered for 2 hours. Puree again and return to heat. Reduce to a thick sauce consistency. Return to blender and, with motor running, slowly drizzle in 1 cup olive oil. Season with salt and pepper to taste, set aside and keep warm.

Cut eggplants in half lengthwise, brush with olive oil and grill. Salt and pepper sea scallops and place on grill. Pour sauce onto warmed plates. Arrange 5 grilled sea scallops around 2 eggplant halves and garnish with cilantro leaves. *Serves 4.*

Reduce olive oil to 2 tablespoons in sauce, and use only 2 teaspoons to grill eggplant. Recipe is high in fiber, vitamin A and folic acid.

Macon-Lundy Les Charmes (French White)
Delaporte Sancerre (French White)

GRILLED VEGETABLE TORTILLA ROLL
with Roasted Jalapeño Mayonnaise

PORK LOIN
with Cactus Pepper Relish and Ancho Chile Sauce

WILD TURKEY ROLL
with Ancho Chile Sweet Corn Sauce

ADOBE CLUB SANDWICH
with Poblano Cilantro Pesto

Have you had your cactus today? Cactus Bar & Grill at the corner of Main and Seventh Streets in downtown Fort Worth showcases Executive Chef Reinhard Warmuth's New Southwest cuisine. Under the Radisson Plaza flag, the Cactus' 1990s reincarnation boasts a menu filled with native Texas ingredients.

Kevin Kelly, Food and Beverage manager says, "Cactus offers great entertainment: a buffet at happy hour, live music on the weekends, and Sunday brunch."

Colorful Southwestern accents abound throughout the vibrantly decorated restaurant. One entire wall resonates with a golden desert mural.

The menu features Warmuth's interpretations of regional favorites. The Stuffed Anaheim Chile is filled with grilled chicken, black beans and chorizo. Grilled vegetables and Jalapeño Garlic Mayonnaise grace the strikingly presented Tortilla Roll. Wild fowl, rabbit, leg of lamb, pork loin, and beef steak vie for diners' attention among traditional entrees. "The food is not spicy, and certainly not overpowering. The chiles and spices add natural excitement and an essence to be savored," says Warmuth. "We use foods low in fat and cholesterol, and no cream products."

"The New Southwest is simple and healthy; a combination of the freshest regional products mixed with peppers, chiles, spices and fresh cactus," Warmuth says. Yes! There is cactus in the items so-titled. No, there aren't any thorns in the food. From Cactus Chowder to Prickly Pear Mousse, the food enjoyed by native Americans for thousands of years debuts in Tarrant County.

Warmuth, a native of Hamburg, Germany, brings years of international experience to his palette of native foodstuffs, and the result is unlike any other cuisine. He has studied and worked from Europe's great culinary centers, to the Caribbean, Denver and Dallas. His Denver apprentices recently sent Warmuth a newspaper article. They won first and second place in a Colorado culinary competition due to Warmuth's tutelage.

Warmuth expresses his culinary philosophy simply, "Go exploring — the world is open."

LIGHTER BITES

Select the Tortilla Roll, Gazpacho, any salad, an Adobe Club, Grilled Chicken Breast, the Sautéed Pork Medallions or Wild Game Pasta, Hickory Smoked Rabbit or Roasted Leg of Lamb. Request dressings on the side.

Radisson Plaza Hotel
815 Main Street
Fort Worth, TX 76102
817/882-1323

GRILLED VEGETABLE TORTILLA ROLL
with Roasted Jalapeño Mayonnaise

Look for this striking appetizer in the "Desert Dining" photograph.

2 zucchini, yellow squash, carrots
  and tomatoes
1 medium red onion
  Herb Oil (recipe follows)
  Salt and pepper
6 10-inch flour tortillas
  Roasted Jalapeño Mayonnaise
  (recipe follows)
1 bunch cilantro, chopped, for garnish

HERB OIL
1/4 cup white wine
1 cup virgin olive oil
1 cup chopped fresh herbs
1 small red onion, diced

ROASTED JALAPEÑO MAYONNAISE
3 jalapeño peppers
1 clove garlic, split and rubbed
  with oil
1 cup extra-virgin olive oil
2 tablespoons Dijon mustard
1 tablespoon lemon juice
  Salt and pepper

Slice vegetables very thinly lengthwise. Marinate in the herb oil for at least two hours. Salt and pepper vegetables and grill. Warm tortillas and spread with roasted jalapeño mayonnaise. Distribute grilled vegetables onto tortillas evenly and roll tightly. Trim ends, and cut on the diagonal into thirds. Place some mayonnaise in a plastic squeeze bottle and draw lines onto plate. Stand tortilla rolls on plate and garnish with chopped cilantro. *Serves 6.*

Puree ingredients in the blender and season with salt and pepper. Yields 2 cups.

Roast jalapeños until the skin blisters. Place in a plastic bag to steam. Peel and seed. Bake garlic clove at 350 degrees until soft and puree with jalapeños and olive oil. Place Dijon mustard and lemon juice in a bowl. Slowly whisk in flavored oil. Yields 1 1/2 cups.

 Use prepared fat-free mayonnaise and flavor with garlic and jalapeño. Recipe is rich in anti-oxidants and folic acid, and high in fiber.

 Rosemount Shiraz (Australian Red)
Slaughter-Leftwich Sauvignon Blanc (Texas White)

PORK LOIN *with Cactus Pepper Relish and Ancho Chile Sauce*

A jar of cactus may be substituted for fresh cactus pads and Knorr brand prepared demi-glace mix for brown sauce.

3 **pounds boneless pork loin**
Cactus Pepper Relish
(recipe follows)
1 1/2 **cups Ancho Chile Sauce**
(recipe follows)

CACTUS PEPPER RELISH

2 **cactus pads**
1 **each green, red, and yellow bell pepper**
1 **small red onion**
2 **tablespoons olive oil**
1 **tablespoon each lemon and lime juice**
1 **bunch cilantro, chopped**
Salt and pepper

ANCHO CHILE SAUCE

1 **red onion, chopped**
1 **clove garlic, minced**
1 **ancho chile, seeded**
2 **tablespoons extra-virgin olive oil**
2 **tablespoons tequila**
1 **sprig each thyme and oregano**
2 **cups brown sauce**
Salt and pepper

Butterfly pork loin by cutting almost through lengthwise. Pound to even thickness. Spread with cactus pepper relish, roll and tie. Roast at 350 degrees until the internal temperature is 155 degrees, about 30 minutes. Wrap in foil for 5 minutes before slicing. Add Ancho Chile Sauce. *Serves 8.*

If using fresh cactus, remove nubs with a vegetable peeler. Roast cactus and peppers at 450 degrees for 30 to 45 minutes or until skin blisters. Place in plastic bag for 10 minutes. Peel, seed, and dice. Place in a bowl with onion. Add olive oil, lemon and lime juices and cilantro. Salt and pepper to taste.

Sauté onion, garlic, and chile in oil until onions are clear. Add tequila and reduce to dry. Add herbs and brown sauce, and simmer for 15 minutes. Blend sauce until smooth. Strain and season. This sauce will keep a week in the refrigerator. Yields 2 cups.

 Omit oil from relish and chile sauce. The loin is the leanest pork cut, and bell peppers are nutrient-rich.

 St. Francis Merlot (California Red)
Badia a Coltibuono Trappolini (Italian White)

WILD TURKEY ROLL *with Sweet Corn Ancho Chile Sauce*

Regular turkey breast may be substituted.

2 **Anaheim peppers**
3 **pounds raw, boneless, skinless**
  wild turkey breast
6 **ounces goat cheese**
1 1/2 **cups Ancho Chile Sweet**
  Corn Sauce
1 **ear sweet corn**

Roast peppers at 450 degrees until the skin blisters. Place in plastic bag for 10 minutes. Peel, seed, dice and blend with goat cheese. Butterfly breast by cutting through almost through lengthwise. Pound to 1/4-inch thickness. Season and spread on cheese mixture. Roll and tie. Bake at 350 degrees until internal temperature is 160 degrees, about 25 minutes. Grill corn and remove kernels. Add to sauce in pork loin recipe. *Serves 6.*

 Omit oil from chile sauce, sauté with Pam, and substitute 4 ounces feta cheese.

 Cap Rock Cabernet Royale (Texas Rose)
Hogue Semillon (Washington White)

ADOBE CLUB SANDWICH *with Poblano Cilantro Pesto*

This sandwich explodes with Southwest flavors.

1 **cup honey**
2 **tablespoons each lemon and**
  lime juice
1/4 **of a habanero or Scotch bonnet chile**
2 **pounds uncooked turkey breast**
12 **pita bread rounds**
1/2 **small lettuce head, shredded**

POBLANO CILANTRO PESTO
2 **fresh poblano peppers**
1 **red onion and 3 cloves garlic**
1 **bunch cilantro**
1 **cup extra-virgin olive oil**
3 **tablespoons white wine**

Mix honey and juices with habanero chile. Marinate thinly sliced turkey in mixture for 2-3 hours. Grill turkey and warm pita bread. Spread pita with pesto, add lettuce and turkey and top with a second pita. Cut into quarters and serve warm. *Makes 6 sandwiches.*

Roast peppers at 450 degrees until the skin blisters. Place in plastic bag for 10 minutes, and peel and seed under running water. Blend with remaining ingredients. Season to taste. *Yields about 2 cups.*

 Honey keeps meat moist and tasty. Reduce oil in pesto to 1/4 cup and use whole-wheat pita bread to add fiber.

 Fall Creek Emerald Riesling (Texas White)
Joseph Phelphs Gewurztraminer (California White)

BEEF TENDERLOIN
with A Gorgonzola and Green Peppercorn Cream Sauce
DIJON VINAIGRETTE
CHOCOLATE VELVET MOUSSE CAKE
CILANTRO AND JALAPEÑO CREAM SAUCE
CAFE MATTHEW TORTILLA SOUP

Indulge in top-notch dining at Sally Bolick's Cafe Matthew in North Richland Hills. The cafe's sleek, contemporary decor is reminiscent of Los Angeles and Miami, but the attitude is pure Texas. Bolick greets patrons at the door with a wide smile and gracious hospitality.

Cafe Matthew's mid-cities magic extends to the kitchen, where chef Jose Rodriguez turns out huge, colorful meals. Entrees arrive at the table with several accompanying dishes, including a creamy potato casserole, warm beets, a deliciously sweet butternut squash puree, and freshly steamed vegetables. The fish entrees are perfectly cooked, and served with light flavorful sauces and salsas.

The house specialties include Poached Norwegian Salmon with Dijon Mustard Cream Sauce, Roast Rack of Lamb with Mixed Herbs and Roasted Garlic Sauce, and Scaloppine of Veal with Port Wine Mushroom Sauce. Delectable desserts such as Strawberries Romanoff and Chocolate Decadence are temptingly displayed in the dining room to remind guests of after-dinner delights.

Lunch is relaxing and friendly at Cafe Matthew. The polished service is soothing, and although orders are filled quickly, it is difficult to leave this restful haven. "Our lunch customers are health-conscious," Bolick says. "We have many noontime requests for low-fat meals. But our dinner crowd is just the opposite — they come to indulge in a great meal."

"Rodriguez is wonderful with flavor, and strives to titillate the customers' tastebuds with touches of the Southwest," Bolick says. The original chef, John Webber, designed the menu, and his influence lingers.

Cafe Matthew's knowledgeable waitstaff is highly trained in food and wine matching. They are very familiar with wine varietals, and can discuss each selection. Bolick reports that three-fourths of the dinner customers order wine.

Cafe Matthew is an oasis in suburbia. The restaurant won several accolades in a recent Fort Worth Star-Telegram readers poll: Best Customer Service, Most Romantic, and Best Restaurant When Someone Else Is Paying.

Old Towne Square
8251 Bedford-Euless Rd.
Suite 231
North Richland Hills, TX
76180-2713
Metro 817/577-3463

LIGHTER BITES

Select Escargot and Angel Hair Pasta With Basil & Tomato (omit cream) or Norwegian Smoked Salmon, Smoked Emu & Spinach Salad With Honey Dressing (omit egg), or Fish Poached In White Wine With Yellow Tomato Salsa.

BEEF TENDERLOIN
with Gorgonzola Cheese and Green Peppercorn Cream Sauce

Texans delight in this serious beef recipe. Pan juices can be substituted for veal stock.

- 1   5-pound beef tenderloin
- 2   tablespoons corn oil
- 3   cups heavy cream
- 1/2 cup white wine
- 1   tablespoon minced shallots
- 2   teaspoons green peppercorns
- 1/2 cup veal stock
- 1   ounce Gorgonzola cheese
     Pinch of salt

Preheat oven to 350 degrees. Sear tenderloin in oil in a large sauté pan for 2 minutes per side to seal in juices. Bake 20 to 25 minutes for medium rare. Remove from oven and cover with foil for 5 to 10 minutes before slicing.

While the tenderloin is cooking, warm the heavy cream, white wine, shallots, peppercorns, veal stock and salt over medium heat. Bring to a boil and cook, stirring often, until sauce has thickened. Just before serving, add gorgonzola and stir until cheese melts. *Serves 8 to 10.*

 Sear meat with 2 teaspoons oil. Substitute evaporated skim milk, and defat stock or drippings.

 Frescobaldi Castello de Nipozzano (Italian Red)
Martinez-Bujanda Gran Reserva (Spanish Red)

DIJON VINAIGRETTE

Create a salad of fresh asparagus spears and baby lettuces to showcase this zippy vinaigrette.

- 1   egg
- 2   teaspoons Dijon mustard
- 1 1/2 cups vegetable oil
- 1   teaspoon lemon juice
- 2   teaspoons red wine vinegar
- 2   teaspoons white wine
- 1/4 teaspoon salt
- 1/4 teaspoon white pepper

Boil egg for 1 minute. In a small bowl, whisk together egg and mustard. Slowly add oil in a steady stream, whisking constantly. Add remaining ingredients and mix well. *Serves 6 to 8.*

 Cambria Chardonnay (California White)
Chalk Hill Chardonnay (California White)

CHOCOLATE VELVET MOUSSE CAKE

This recipe is from a special customer who loves the dessert, but prefers that someone else make it.

- 1 **pound semi-sweet chocolate**
- 2 **whole eggs**
- 4 **egg yolks**
- 2 **cups heavy cream**
- 6 **tablespoons confectioners' sugar**
- 1 **cup egg white**
- 1/4 **cup grated white chocolate**

CRUST
- 1 **9-ounce box chocolate wafers**
- 1/2 **cup butter, melted**

Melt semi-sweet chocolate in double-boiler over simmering water. Cool slightly. Add whole eggs and yolks and mix thoroughly. Whip cream with sugar until stiff. Whip egg whites to medium-stiff peaks. Gently fold whipped cream and egg whites alternately into melted chocolate mixture.

Crush chocolate wafers in food processor. Add melted butter and combine. Press crust mixture into bottom of a 10-inch spring-form pan. Top with chocolate mousse. Refrigerate for 2 hours. Top with grated white chocolate. *Serves 10 to 12.*

 Substitute egg substitutes for whole eggs, 4 cups Cool Whip, 1/4 cup margarine, and use only 1/8 cup white chocolate.

 Ferrari Brut Perle (Italian Sparkling Wine)
Moet & Chandon Brut Imperial (French Champagne)
Chateau Monbazillac (French Dessert Wine)

CILANTRO AND JALAPEÑO CREAM SAUCE

This classic sauce with Southwestern flair was created by Chef Rodriguez. Cafe Matthew serves it with Sautéed Gulf Shrimp and Fettucini.

- 1 **teaspoon minced garlic**
- 1 **teaspoon olive oil**
- 1 **cup dry white wine**
- 4 **cups heavy cream**
- 2 **teaspoons finely chopped fresh jalapeños**
- 1/2 **cup coarsely chopped cilantro**
- 1/2 **cup diced tomato**

In a heavy skillet over medium-low heat, sauté garlic in oil until golden. Add wine and simmer 10 minutes. Slowly drizzle heavy cream into skillet. Simmer, stirring often, until reduced by half, about 30 minutes. Just before serving, add jalapeño, cilantro and tomato and cook until hot. *Serves 6 to 8.*

 Substitute evaporated skim milk to sharply reduce calories.

 Mastroberardino Greco di Tufo (Italian White)
Lindeman Padthaway Sauvignon Blanc (Australian White)

CAFE MATTHEW TORTILLA SOUP

This soup is quite fiery. To reduce the heat, seed the pepper or use half a jalapeño.

    2 tablespoons olive oil
    4 medium tomatoes, chopped
    1/2 medium onion, chopped
    4 corn tortillas, quartered
    1 jalapeño, diced
    2 tablespoons chopped fresh cilantro
    6 cups chicken stock
    1/2 teaspoon ground cumin
    1/2 teaspoon salt
      White pepper

GARNISH
      Avocado slices
      Hard-boiled eggs
      Shredded Monterey Jack or
        Jarlsberg cheese
      Fried corn tortilla strips

Sauté tomatoes, onion, tortillas, jalapeño and cilantro in olive oil in a heavy pan. Cook until tortillas and tomatoes are soft. Add chicken stock and seasonings. Bring to a boil, reduce heat and simmer for 20 minutes.

Puree soup in small batches. Strain. Reheat and serve with avocado, eggs, cheese and tortilla strips. *Serves 6.*

 Sauté with 1 teaspoon olive oil and use only 1 teaspoon salt. For garnish, use 6 tablespoons avocado and 12 tablespoons reduced-fat cheese. Omit egg yolk and fried tortilla strips.

 Fall Creek Chardonnay (Texas White)
Montevina Fumé Blanc (California White)

FACING PAGE
The New West
*Jean-Claude Adam, left,
Hans Bergmann, Carlo Crocci,
Gerard Bahon.*

FOLLOWING PAGE
Desert Dining
*Mary Swift, left, Reinhard Warmuth,
Willis McIntosh, Sally Bolick.*

GRILLED PORTABELLA MUSHROOMS AND ROASTED RED BELL PEPPERS

MR. MAC'S SALAD DRESSING

SALMON
with Tomato-Basil Vinaigrette and Sauteed Spinach

ESPRESSO TORTE

FIVE ONION SOUP

Memories of perfectly cooked Chateaubriand, Lemon Sole, Mac's Salad with Marinated Shrimp, and Escargot in Garlic Butter are part of a Fort Worth legend. Special friends and romantic dinners accompany thoughts of Carriage House hospitality. Today, people can still enjoy the result of restaurateur Willis McIntosh's thirty-plus years of hands-on experience in his Fort Worth restaurants.

McIntosh entered the food industry as a butcher at Roy Pope Grocery in 1948. He opened the Carriage House in 1959 to fill a void in West Side restaurants. "All we really wanted was to be able to get a good steak on Camp Bowie," he says. He was successful. The rest is history.

The Carriage House

"I'm changing my concept some," McIntosh says. "I've brought a team of talented young chefs into the kitchen. They have a new and inspired attitude concerning Fort Worth cuisine. They are updating half of the menu, and offering new specials every night," he says.

Kimberly McIntosh, a third-generation restaurateur, manages The Carriage House. She emphasizes that people are eating more sensibly and are attracted to regional ingredients. Grilled Portabella Mushrooms, Chicken and Penne Pasta, and Tequila and Lime Marinated Chicken with Grilled Vegetables are favorites.

mac's house
Restaurant & Tavern

If Carriage House formality isn't necessary, find Mac's House at Forest Park and Park Hill. Manager Tim Johnson welcomes customers to a neighborhood hideaway. Menu choices from Stuffed Flounder to Chicken Cordon Bleu to Kansas City Strip Sirloin have become Fort Worth classics. Leroy Nieman sports-theme prints hang in one room and hunting scene prints in another. In contrast, the Carriage House bar is adorned with McIntosh's "girls," the first nudes in Fort Worth publicly displayed, except in an art museum.

At either restaurant, end the evening with a Brandy Ice — McIntosh's decadent dessert drink is the best way to sweeten any memory.

CARRIAGE HOUSE
5136 Camp Bowie Blvd.
Fort Worth, TX 76107
817/732-2873

——————— LIGHTER BITES ———————

Carriage House: Crab Cakes with lemon or picante sauces, the Mixed Grill, or Dover Sole with sauce on the side are good choices.

Mac's House: Try Grilled Catfish without butter, half orders of Eggs Benedict (sauce on the side) or Baked Chicken.

MAC'S HOUSE
2400 Park Hill Drive
Fort Worth, TX 76110
817/921-4682

GRILLED PORTABELLA MUSHROOMS *with Roasted Red Bell Peppers*

This is a wonderful vegetarian dish.

MUSHROOMS
 4 medium portabella mushrooms
 1 cup extra-virgin olive oil
 1/2 cup butter, melted
 1 head garlic, finely chopped
 3 tablespoons fresh rosemary minced
   Salt and white pepper
   Garnish of rosemary sprigs,

PEPPERS
 2 red bell peppers
 1 tablespoon extra-virgin olive oil
 1 teaspoon red wine vinegar
 1/2 clove garlic, minced
   Pinch minced fresh herbs

Season mushrooms with salt and white pepper. Marinate in olive oil, butter, garlic and rosemary for at least 30 minutes. Grill about 10 minutes, turning once.

Char peppers on grill until skin is blackened. Place peppers in a plastic bag or paper sack for 15 minutes. Remove skin from peppers, cut in half, and remove seeds and stem. Season peppers with remaining ingredients and serve with mushrooms. *Serves 4.*

Sauté in Pam plus 1 teaspoon olive oil and 1 teaspoon butter. Cut salt to a pinch, and use just 2 teaspoons oil on peppers.

Chateau de la Maltroye (French Red)
Kenwood Pinot Noir (California Red)

MR. MAC'S SALAD

A classic at The Carriage House for 20 years.

 1 cup lemon juice
 1 teaspoon Lawry's seasoned pepper
 1/2 teaspoon dry mustard
 1/2 teaspoon salt
 1 teaspoon freshly ground pepper
 1 tablespoon Worcestershire sauce
   Dash Tabasco sauce
 1/4 cup grated onion
 1 hard cooked egg, grated
 2 cups safflower oil
 1/2 pound mushrooms, sliced
 2 cups grated Swiss cheese

Combine lemon juice, seasoned pepper, mustard, salt and pepper, Worcestershire, Tabasco, onion and egg. Add oil in a thin steady stream while mixing constantly with a whisk. Makes 3 1/2 cups.

Tear Romaine, Bibb and Radichio lettuces into bite sized pieces and toss with mushrooms, cheese and dressing. *Serves 12.*

Recipe is rich in vitamins A and B, calcium, magnesium and folic acid. Omit salt and egg, and use just 1 cup Swiss and 1 cup oil to cut fat and calories by half.

Franco Fiorina Gavi (Italian White)
Alexander Valley Chardonnay (California White)

SALMON *with Tomato-Basil Vinaigrette & Sautéed Spinach*

One of the new tastes at The Carriage House.

SALMON
  4 **6-ounce salmon fillets**
1/2 **cup melted butter**
1/3 **cup white wine**
    Juice of 1 lemon
    Salt and pepper

SAUTÉED SPINACH
1/4 **cup olive oil**
  2 **cloves garlic**
1/2 **pound fresh spinach**
    Salt and pepper

TOMATO-BASIL VINAIGRETTE
  1 **tablespoon Dijon mustard**
  2 **lemons, juiced**
  2 **tablespoons balsamic vinegar**
  2 **tablespoons white wine vinegar**
    Salt and freshly ground black pepper
3/4 **cup olive oil**
  3 **tomatoes, cored, peeled,
    seeded and chopped**
  3 **tablespoons chopped fresh basil**
  2 **green onions, sliced**

Place salmon in a shallow pan. Add butter, wine, and lemon juice. Season with salt and pepper. Broil until fish is no longer transparent, about 10 minutes.

While the fish is broiling, heat a large skillet. Add olive oil, garlic and fresh spinach. Sauté until spinach is just wilted. Season with salt and pepper.

To prepare the dressing, combine Dijon mustard, lemon juice, vinegars, salt and pepper. Slowly drizzle in olive oil, whisking constantly. Then add remaining ingredients and mix well. Vinaigrette should be made 4 hours in advance to allow flavors to blend.

To serve, divide spinach among 4 plates. Place salmon fillet on bed of spinach and top with tomato basil vinaigrette. *Serves 4.*

 Recipe is wonderfully nutrient-rich. Sauté salmon without butter or salt, use just 1 teaspoon oil in spinach and 3 teaspoons in dressing. Use only 1/4 teaspoon salt in vinaigrette.

 Merryvale Meritage (California White)
Les Vieux Cepage Le Tresor (California Red)

ESPRESSO TORTE

This is a decadent, pudding-like torte.

       1   **pound butter**
       1   **cup each sugar and espresso**
     12   **ounces bittersweet chocolate,
             chopped**
       4   **ounces unsweetened chocolate,
             chopped**
       8   **large eggs, beaten
             Garnish of strawberry puree and
             confectioner's sugar**

 eat butter, sugar and espresso in saucepan until butter is melted. Do not boil. Add chopped chocolate and heat gently until chocolate is melted. Do not boil. Remove from heat and whisk in beaten eggs. Pour into a greased and floured foil-lined 9x3-inch springform pan. Bake at 350 degrees for 55 to 60 minutes. When cooled, remove from pan and slice. Garnish on a pool of strawberry puree. Sprinkle with confectioners sugar. *Serves 12 -16.*

Orlando Carrington Extra Brut (Australian Sparkling Wine)
Pol Roget Brut (French Champagne)

FIVE ONION SOUP

For rich flavor cook the onions long and slow.

       6   **tablespoons butter**
       1   **cup sliced white onion**
       1   **cup sliced yellow onion**
       4   **leeks (white part only), sliced**
    1/2   **cup sliced shallots**
       6   **cloves garlic**
    1/4   **cup sherry**
       4   **cups chicken stock**
       1   **teaspoon fresh thyme, minced**
       1   **bay leaf**
       1   **cup heavy cream**
    1/4   **cup sliced scallions**
       6   **toasted croutons
             Shredded provolone and Parmesan**

 elt butter in a large soup pot. Add onions, leeks, shallots and garlic and cook over low heat until vegetables are lightly colored, about 20 minutes. Add sherry, stock, thyme and bay leaf. Bring to a boil, reduce heat and simmer for 20 minutes. Let cool slightly and puree in a blender or food processor.

Reheat and add cream and scallions. Ladle into individual ovenproof serving bowls. Top with croutons and cheeses. Place soup under broiler to melt cheese. Serve immediately. *Serves 6.*

 Use just 1 tablespoon butter plus 1 tablespoon olive oil, use evaporated skim milk, just 2 ounces Parmesan and 1 ounce provolone, and toast croutons without butter.

Valdespino Fino (Spanish Sherry)
Napa Ridge Sauvignon Blanc (California White)

CHICKEN SOUP
with Kreplach

CARSHON BARS

REUBEN SANDWICH

STUFFED CABBAGE

FRENCH COCONUT PIE

Carshon's Delicatessen is proof that an eatery doesn't have to be Western to hold a place in Cowtown tradition. The establishment has been serving kosher-style Yankee sandwiches in Fort Worth since it opened downtown in 1928.

In fact, it has so much tradition that owner Mary Swift says she can date returning patrons by their memories of the deli — whether it be the location or the specials. A wealth of memories exist from the 65-year history of this local meeting place.

Old-fashioned simplicity reigns in the current location on Cleburne Road, where Carshon's moved in the early 70s. The unassuming building and its clean, white walls decked in vintage sepia-tone prints surround the real Carshon's tradition, its customers. For generations, people of all walks of life, wearing anything from overalls to Armani, have frequented this lunchtime haven. And while faces have changed over the years, the deli's reputation has not.

When Swift has time, she enjoys cooking and creating the blackboard specials. She has adapted the menu slightly to meet the demands of a changing lunch crowd. "We are serving more turkey and lighter sandwiches and offering more salads," Swift says. "Customers consider it splurging to order a whole sandwich."

Tradition remains in Carshon's menu, as well. The spread of "R"-named sandwiches — Rutherford, Rachel, Rebecca, Ruthie and Reuben — are still deli staples with a side order of potato salad or beans. Home-style soups include Matzo Ball, Kreplach, and Split Pea. To finish the meal, suggestions are "Strawberry Delight," Homemade Cheesecake, or Internationally Famous Pie. For those who mark their calendars by Carshon's pie of the day, it is Lemon or Butterscotch on Tuesday, Chocolate on Wednesday and Saturday, Coconut on Thursday and Banana on Friday.

Co-owner Dennis Swift seeks out unusual beers and exceptional wines to offer by the glass. Also available are limited kosher meats and cheeses for traditional Jewish dishes.

Life is all about good food and fond memories. At Carshon's the two go hand-in-hand.

LIGHTER BITES

Order a roast beef or turkey sandwich, Chicken Noodle or Bean and Barley Soup, or the fish plate with tuna, salmon or sardines (omit egg). Beans or tomato slices are good side orders.

3133 Cleburne Road
Fort Worth, TX 76110
817/923-1907

CHICKEN SOUP *with Kreplach*

Fry the kreplach dumplings and serve as an hors d'oeuvre.

SOUP
- 1 **5-pound hen**
- 16 **cups water**
- 2 **cups chopped onion**
- 2 **cups chopped carrots**
- 2 **cups chopped celery, with leaves**
- 1 **tablespoon salt**
- 1 **teaspoon white pepper**

KREPLACH
- 1 **cup cooked chicken**
- 1/4 **cup diced onion**
- 4 **eggs (divided use)**
- 2 **tablespoons water**
- 1 **teaspoon Lawry's seasoning salt**
  White pepper
- 2 **cups flour**

Wash hen and remove any excess fat. Place it in a large stock pot and add water to cover. Add vegetables and seasoning and bring to a boil. Reduce heat and simmer until chicken is tender, about 1 hour. Bone the chicken. Return bones to pot and cook 3 to 4 hours. Strain and cool. Refrigerate overnight. Skim congealed fat from top of broth.

Dice 2 cups chicken and add to broth. Float 4 to 5 kreplach in soup. Use remaining cooked chicken in kreplach, a salad or a casserole. *Serves 8.*

Grind together the chicken, onion and one egg. Add seasoning salt and white pepper. Set filling aside.

Place flour in one pile on a pastry board. Make a well in the center and break 3 eggs into the well. Add water and incorporate flour a bit at a time until all flour is mixed in. If dough is too dry, a little more water may be beaten in. Dough should form a manageable ball with no dry places. Knead dough until it holds together and becomes flexible. This can be done in a food processor.

Work with one fourth of the dough at a time, keeping the rest covered so it doesn't dry out. Roll out the dough until you can see through it. Cut the rolled dough into 3-inch squares and fill with 1 tablespoon chicken filling. Fold over diagonally, seal the edges with water, and press into a triangle.

Cook in simmering stock or water for 10 minutes, until kreplach float. Rinse with cold water to stop cooking. Drain well and let dry. Freeze individually on baking sheet. Heat in soup. *Yields 5 dozen.*

 Mirassou Dry Chenin Blanc (California White)
Villa Mt. Eden Chardonnay (California White)

CARSHON BARS

This dessert is perfect for a family reunion.

  2 cups chocolate chips
  1 can Eagle Brand sweetened
    condensed milk
  2 tablespoons margarine
1/4 teaspoon salt
  1 cup chopped nuts
  1 teaspoon vanilla
  1 cup butter or margarine
  2 cups brown sugar, packed
  2 eggs
  2 teaspoons vanilla
2 1/4 cups flour
  1 teaspoon baking soda
  1 teaspoon salt
  4 cups rolled oats

For filling, combine chocolate chips, condensed milk, margarine and salt over low heat. Stir until smooth and add nuts and vanilla. Set aside and keep warm.

To make the crust, combine remaining ingredients thoroughly. Place one fourth of the crust mixture in bottom of each of two 8 1/2x11-inch cake pans and pat smooth. Pour chocolate mixture over it evenly, then add remaining crust mixture in small dots. Bake at 325 degrees for 25 minutes. *Yields 32 bars.*

 Omit margarine from filling. For crust, reduce nuts to 1/4 cup, use only 1/4 cup margarine, egg substitute and reduce salt to 1/2 teaspoon.

 Chateau LaTour Blanche (French Dessert Wine)

REUBEN SANDWICH

A crisp pickle and cold salad are ideal complements.

    Sauerkraut, drained
  4 teaspoons butter
  4 slices rye bread
2/3 pound sliced corned beef
  2 ounces sliced Swiss cheese

Warm sauerkraut. Butter one side of each piece of bread. Assemble corned beef and cheese between slices and grill until meat and cheese are warmed through. Remove from grill, open sandwich and add sauerkraut. *Serves 2.*

 Grill bread without butter, use only 3 ounces corned beef and substitute reduced-fat cheese.

 Lorinon Crianza (Spanish Red)
Antinori Santa Cristina (Italian Red)

STUFFED CABBAGE

This is a smaller version of corned beef and cabbage.

- 1 head green cabbage
- 1 pound ground beef or turkey
- 1/4 cup uncooked rice
- 1/2 teaspoon salt
- 3/4 cup brown sugar
- 1 teaspoon sour salt (citric acid)
- 1 8-ounce can tomato sauce
- 1/2 cup boiling water
- 3/4 cup sauerkraut with some juice

Boil cabbage and remove 12 large outer leaves. Shred remaining leaves and place in a large shallow dish. Combine meat with rice. Place 2 tablespoons in each cabbage leaf. Roll the leaves up and tuck in the ends. Sprinkle salt, sugar and sour salt over cabbage rolls. Add tomato sauce, water and sauerkraut. Extra liquid may be added if the dish is to be reheated. Bake covered at 350 degrees for 1 1/2 to 2 hours, basting occasionally. *Serves 6.*

 Substitute ground turkey breast, omit sour salt and use brown rice and unsalted tomato sauce.

 Marques de Caceres Reserva (Spanish Red)
Nobilo Sauvignon Blanc (New Zealand White)

FRENCH COCONUT PIE

This and pear pie are the cook's favorites.

FILLING
- 1 cup soft butter
- 3 cups sugar
- 6 eggs
- 4 tablespoons vinegar
- 2 teaspoons vanilla
- 1 cup coconut

CRUST
- 4 cups flour
- 2 teaspoons salt
- 1 1/2 cups shortening
- 2/3 cup water

To prepare the filling, cream butter and sugar. Beat in eggs and add vinegar and vanilla. Mix well. Make the pie crust by mixing flour and salt. Cut in shortening. Add water slowly while mixing dough. Divide in half and roll each piece to a 1/4-inch thick sheet. Press into 2 9-inch pie plates and trim edges.

Place half of the coconut in each unbaked pie shell. Add filling mixture and bake at 350 degrees for 1 hour. *Yields 2 pies.*

 Substitute 1/2 cup margarine for butter and 3/4 cup margarine for shortening, use 1 1/2 cups egg substitute, reduce coconut to 1/4 cup and salt to 1 1/2 teaspoons.

 Benziger Blanc de Blancs (California Sparkling Wine)
Mumm Cuvee Napa Brut Prestige (California Sparkling Wine)

HUEVOS RANCHEROS

CARNE ASADA

MIGAS

GUACAMOLE

SALSA DE TOMATE VERDE CON AGUACATE

SOPA DE TORTILLA

Buenos dias, mis amigos! Entre en el paradiso. Step through the main door of Joe T. Garcia's landmark restaurant, or through the stone archway into a garden of lush, tropical plants. Stroll along the bricked patio to a table by the pool, or choose one by the foliage for more intimacy. Listen as the mariachi band plays "las favoritos canciónes de Mexicanos."

The sights and smells are reminiscent of Old Mexico as are the foods and flavors. The menu includes fajitas and margaritas, nachos and enchiladas, and a combination plate known as "The Dinner."

In addition to Joe T. Garcia's restaurant, there are also two bakeries. At the bustling North Main Street bakery, nicknamed Esperanza's, Hope Garcia Lancarte arrives before the sun rises each morning. She is the leader of three generations of the Garcia family and the force behind the empire. Her energy and presence are readily apparent as she greets regulars and newcomers and personally oversees the preparation and presentation of the generous food platters.

Joe T. Garcia's Mexican Bakery on Hemphill is managed by the watchful eyes of Jesse Lancarte. The bakeries serve breakfast foods all day and also offer a lunch menu. Both have deli cases full of roasted meats, maza, and a variety of Mexican pastries.

The original restaurant's patio and pool area now seats 500, making it the largest al fresco dining area in the Southwest. The Garcias are bottling their salsa picante, so the family's flavor is available at home to accompany the wonderful recipes on the following pages.

Sound like a lot? For Mrs. Garcia Lancarte it is all a part of running the family business. She admits that what is good for the family is generally good for business. And that's the other part of her job — making sure things stay that way.

"I try to keep the family united and goal-oriented," she says. "And, I give them a lot of love, too."

JOE T. GARCIA'S
RESTAURANT
2201 North Commerce
Fort Worth, TX 76106
817/626-4356

JOE T. GARCIA'S
BAKERIES
2140 North Main Street
Fort Worth, TX 76106
817/626-5770

1109 Hemphill
Fort Worth, TX 76104
817/332-3848

──────── LIGHTER BITES ────────

Choose grilled chicken salad, or chicken or beef fajitas without added oil or guacamole. Skip fried chips, and try salsa on flour tortillas instead.

SALSA DE TOMATE VERDE CON AGUACATE
(Green Tomato & Avocado Salsa)

Tomatillos are generally used while green and quite firm. Their flavor has hints of lemon, apple and herbs.

  6 serrano chiles
1 1/2 pounds tomatillos, husked
  4 garlic cloves, peeled
  1 teaspoon salt
1/2 cup chopped cilantro
  2 avocados, pitted, peeled and diced
1 1/4 cups minced onion

Place chiles in a large pan of boiling water and cook 5 minutes. Add tomatillos and boil for 3 more minutes. Remove from heat and drain. Puree chiles, tomatillos and garlic. Add salt and cilantro and blend until smooth. Refrigerate. Stir in avocado and onion just before serving. *Yields about 3 cups.*

 DeLoach White Zinfandel (California Blush)
Cune Imperial Gran Reserva Rioja (Spanish Red)

SOPA DE TORTILLA

This comforting soup is nutritious and delicious.

  2 ripe tomatoes, chopped
1/2 onion, chopped
  2 cloves garlic, peeled and crushed
  3 tablespoons lard, plus 1/2 pound
  6 cups chicken broth
  2 small sprigs epazote (optional)
    Salt and pepper
  1 dozen day-old corn tortillas
  2 pasilla chiles (dried)
  3 avocados, pitted, peeled and chopped
  7 ounces queso Chihuahua, grated
    (Mexican cheese)
  2 limes, quartered

Blend tomatoes, onion and garlic in processor and cook in 3 tablespoons lard for 10 minutes, until sauce has thickened. Add chicken broth, epazote, season, and bring to a boil and cook covered over medium heat for 15 minutes.

Heat remaining lard in a skillet. Cut tortillas into thin strips and fry a few at a time, turning at least once, for 3 to 4 minutes or until golden brown. Drain. Cut chiles into thin rings and remove seeds. Fry for 1 minute, and drain. To serve, reheat soup and add tortilla strips. Garnish with avocado, queso Chihuahua, chile rings and fresh lime. *Serves 6.*

 Bake tortillas with Pam, substitute 1 teaspoon vegetable oil for lard to cook sauce and fry chiles. Use reduced-fat Monterey Jack cheese, and garnish with just 1 tablespoon avocado.

 Trimbach Gewurztraminer (French White)
Grape Creek Fumé Blanc (Texas White)

HUMMUS

KIBBI

ABLAMA

TABBULI

MAHSHE WARAK ARESH

Far from the sun-drenched shores of the Eastern Mediterranean, the Hedary family's native Lebanese cuisine delights local adventurers with wholesome Middle Eastern fare.

"Lebanon is the paradise of the Middle East," Marios Hedary says. "Its cuisine is a specialty. It is healthy and different from other food in its use of grains and spices. Our dishes are prepared with the very freshest ingredients."

The family owned a successful restaurant in Beirut for 35 years. The senior Antoine Hedary created all of the recipes, and each of his nine children have worked in the business. George Hedary directs the kitchen at their namesake restaurant in Ridglea. "Our food takes many long hours to prepare, because we cut our own meat and use traditional Lebanese methods of cooking," he says. "We even grow our own grape leaves and herbs for the restaurant."

Hedary's has long been famous for two items. Frarej, chicken baked with potatoes and ripe tomatoes, is a fragrant meal with olive oil, garlic and lemon juice. Samak Mishwi is a baby red snapper rubbed with olive oil and baked, and served with sesame oil, parsley and lemon.

Marios Hedary struck out on his own to open Byblos, named after the charming seaside community and ancient Middle East ruins. Here butter-colored brick walls, and bowls of fresh fruits and vegetables, lend the Mediterranean glow to this North Main location, and a brick oven turns out beautifully crusted Lebanese breads and pizza. "Bread (khubz) makes the whole menu work," Marios Hedary says. "Fresh, hot bread baked in front of you is part of our success."

The Hedarys moved to Fort Worth in 1976 when ethnic food was a rare treat. Locals felt fortunate then to have the original Lebanese fare on White Settlement Road. They showed ongoing appreciation in the Fort Worth Star-Telegram 1993 readers poll by naming Hedary's the "Best Ethnic (Non-Mexican) Restaurant in Tarrant County."

HEDARY'S
3308 Fairfield Avenue
Fort Worth, TX 76116
817/731-6961

———————————— LIGHTER BITES ————————————

Stuffed Summer Squash, Tabbuli, Chopped Tomato or Lettuce Salad (easy on oil) are starters of merit. Baked Chicken, Baby Red Snapper, Stuffed Grape Leaves, Shisk Kabob, or Lamb Chops fill the bill for low-fat dining.

BYBLOS
1406 North Main Street
Fort Worth, TX 76106
817/625-9667

HUMMUS (Garbanzo Bean Dip)

Tahini, available in imported food stores, is a thick paste made of ground sesame seed.

> 2 tablespoons mashed garlic
> 1 tablespoon salt
> 1 1/2 pounds canned, cooked
>   garbanzo beans
> 1 cup sesame paste (tahini)
> 1 cup freshly squeezed lemon juice
> 2 tablespoons olive oil
>   Pita bread

Mash garlic and salt together. Add garbanzo beans, sesame paste, and half the lemon juice. Puree thoroughly with remaining lemon juice. To serve, spread hummus in a thick layer on a small plate. Pour olive oil over hummus. Garnish with radishes, pickled cucumber, turnip and parsley and serve with warm pita bread. *Serves 6 to 8.*

 Use only 1/2 cup tahini, 1/2 cup lemon juice, 1/2 teaspoon salt, and omit olive oil.

 Gonzalez Byass Tio Pepe Fino (Spanish Sherry)
Siglo Rioja Reserva (Spanish Red)

KIBBI (Spiced Ground Lamb)

Kibbi is a basic ingredient for at least ten different Lebanese dishes.

> 1 1/2 cups cracked wheat (bulghur)
> 2 pounds raw ground lamb
> 1 teaspoon salt
> 1/2 teaspoon ground black pepper
> 1/2 cup diced white onions
> 1/4 cup fresh mint leaves
> 1/2 jalapeno pepper, seeded

Soak cracked wheat in water for 15 minutes. Drain away excess water. Mix with the lamb, salt and pepper. Using a fine blade on meat grinder, grind the lamb mixture with remaining ingredients. Pat the mix together into a ball. It can be shaped into patties and charbroiled, or stuffed with sautéed onions and ground sirloin and deep fried. Serve with pita bread. *Serves 8.*

 Ruffino Chianti Classico (Italian Red)
Chalone Pinot Noir (California Red)

BYBLOS ABLAMA *(Stuffed Summer Squash)*

Ablama is a well-balanced one-dish meal.

- 1 pound ground beef or lamb
- 1 small onion, chopped
- 1/2 cup pine nuts
- 1 teaspoon salt
- 1/2 teaspoon black pepper
- 8 medium yellow squash
  Olive oil
- 8 medium tomatoes, diced

Brown ground meat. Add onion, pine nuts, salt and pepper. Set aside to cool. Cut off the tops and core each squash. Discard seeds. Sauté squash until light brown. Stuff squash with meat mixture. Place stuffed squash in a low-sided pan and sprinkle with the diced tomatoes. Bake at 350 degrees for 20 minutes. Serve with rice. *Serves 4 to 6.*

 Use just 2 tablespoons pine nuts, 1/4 teaspoon salt, and sauté with 2 teaspoons oil.

 Jean Leon Chardonnay (Spanish White)
Marques de Arienzo Cosecha Rioja (Spanish Red)

TABBULI *(Cracked Wheat Salad)*

Serve as an appetizer with fresh grape leaves and pita bread.

- 1/2 cup cracked wheat (bulghur)
- 2 bunches green onions, minced
- 1 1/2 teaspoons salt
- 1/4 teaspoon black pepper
- 6 medium tomatoes, finely diced
- 4 bunches parsley, stems removed, minced
- 1/3 cup fresh lemon juice
- 1/4 cup extra-virgin olive oil
  Romaine lettuce and pita bread

Soak cracked wheat in cold water for 15 minutes. Mix with onions, salt and pepper in a large bowl. Add the tomatoes, parsley, and lemon juice and mix well. Add olive oil as desired to each individual serving of tabbuli. Serve with Romaine lettuce and pita bread. *Serves 6.*

 Use just 1 tablespoon oil and 1/2 teaspoon salt.

 Dry Creek Vineyards Dry Chenin Blanc (California White)
Boutari Kretikos (Greek White)

MAHSHE WARAK ARESH (*Stuffed Grape Leaves*)

The Hedary family serves this before a traditional American Thanksgiving.

1 **pound raw ground lamb**
1 **cup cooked rice**
1/2 **tablespoon cinnamon**
1 **tablespoon salt**
1 **teaspoon ground black pepper**
1/3 **cup water**
  About 35 grape leaves
  (available in jars)

SAUCE
6 **cloves garlic, crushed**
1/2 **teaspoon ground dried mint**
1/4 **teaspoon salt**
1/4 **cup freshly squeezed lemon juice**
  Plain yogurt for dipping

Mix together all lamb ingredients except grape leaves. Rinse leaves thoroughly. Lay one leaf at a time on a flat surface and put about 1 tablespoon of the lamb mixture in the middle of the grape leaf. Using your fingers, form the mixture into a sausage shape, and fold the leaf on the right and left sides. Then roll the leaf, shaping it into a cigar.

Place rolled grape leaves into a deep pot, laying them side by side tightly and eventually having two or three layers. Fill pot with water until it covers the top layer of grape leaves and place a heavy dish (about the diameter of the pot) upside down on the grape leaves. Simmer over low heat for 25 minutes.

Remove plate. Mix the sauce ingredients together and pour them onto the grape leaves while still in the pot. Add more water to cover the top layer of grape leaves. Cover and cook without the plate for 10 more minutes. Serve with plain yogurt. *Serves 4.*

 Use only 1/2 teaspoon salt.

 Freixenet Cordon Negro Brut Cava (Spanish Sparkling Wine)
Zaca Mesa Pinot Noir (California Red)

FACING PAGE
Party on the Patio
Franco Hedary, left, Bill Davis, Hope Garcia Lancarte

FOLLOWING PAGE
Artists at Work
Renie Steves, left, Patrick Esquerré, Shelby Schafer

OLIVE SOUP

BUTTERMILK PIE

HOLIDAY ROAST

PECAN PIE

KING RANCH CASSEROLE

TWO-MINUTE MICROWAVE FUDGE

The 1896 Tarantula Train's distinctive whistle can be heard all through Fort Worth, recalling the steam engine days of rail travel. At the end of the line is the Iron Horse Cafe in the Stockyards Station Market, where passengers disembark into the Old West.

Philanthropists Bill and Mitzi Davis, through the Tarantula Corporation, have brought short-haul passenger service to Fort Worth. From the depot at Eighth Avenue, the train takes riders along tracks traveled for generations into the historic Fort Worth Stockyards. Once cattle, sheep and pigs were unloaded here, and sold at daily auctions. People swarmed along the brick-paved street, toward the huge packing houses of Armour and Swift, or to the saloons, restaurants and hotels along Main Street.

The Iron Horse Cafe sits amidst four weather-proof acres of unique shops, galleries and restaurants on Exchange Avenue near North Main Street.

The cafe is reminiscent of the diners which served travelers at city depots when trains paused to take on passengers and freight. Its patio bar opens onto Exchange, affording patrons a view of passengers and passers-by.

Hearty home-cooked meals and Southern hospitality attract travelers, business people, and cowpokes to the cafe. Cliff Cline, Tarantula operations director, describes the daily menu of homemade plate lunches as "good 'ole Southern fare." Lemon Pepper Cod Fish served with Fried Okra, Meat Loaf, Fried Chicken, Pepper Steak and other satisfying bites are offered on a rotating basis. Selections can be made from the soup and salad bar for a fast nutritious lunch. Traditional Peach Cobbler and a selection of pies from Lemon Meringue to Chocolate or Coconut Cream answer the call for a sweet. The patio offers all this plus several additional items for evening customers seeking weekend entertainment.

The Iron Horse Cafe and Tarantula Train can create special events, too. Cline can arrange a banquet at the restaurant or a buffet on the train, and will even stage a good old-fashioned train robbery en route.

LIGHTER BITES

Salad bars offer a wonderful array of meals. Choose fresh, raw vegetables and fruits dressed with lemon juice, vinegar or picante sauce. Select a broth or tomato-based soup. Skip olives, cheese, prepared salads and nuts.

Stockyards Station
140 East Exchange Ave.
Fort Worth, TX 76106
817/625-5520

OLIVE SOUP

This deliciously different warm soup is great as a meal or an appetizer.

          3 tablespoons butter
          3 tablespoons all-purpose flour
          4 cups chicken stock
             Freshly ground black pepper
          1 cup minced ripe black olives
          1 cup heavy cream
             Pinch of salt
       1/4 cup dry sherry
          1 large green onion, minced

Melt butter in saucepan. Blend in the flour and cook over moderate heat, stirring, for 2 minutes. Whisk in the stock and bring to a simmer. Stir in the olives and cream and bring mixture back to a simmer. Add salt if necessary. Stir in the sherry and green onions. *Serves 4 to 6.*

 Substitute skim milk thickened with cornstarch or evaporated skim milk for the cream, and margarine for the butter to cut fat in half and reduce cholesterol to almost zero.

 Freemark Abbey Cabernet Sauvignon (California Red)
Chateau Souverain Cabernet Sauvignon (California Red)

BUTTERMILK PIE

This Southern favorite will melt in your mouth.

          3 egg yolks
    1 1/4 cups sugar
       1/4 cup flour
       1/4 teaspoon salt
          2 cups buttermilk
       1/4 cup butter, melted
          2 teaspoons lemon extract
          1 unbaked 9-inch deep-dish pie shell

Beat egg yolks slightly. Mix in remaining ingredients and pour into unbaked pie shell. Bake in 425-degree oven for 10 minutes. Reduce heat to 325 degrees for 40 minutes, or until a toothpick inserted comes out clean. Let cool thoroughly before serving. *Serves 6 to 8.*

 Substitute margarine for butter and lower the fat and cholesterol. Buttermilk is already low in fat. This pie is very rich in folic acid.

 Segura Viudas Aria Brut Cava (Spanish Sparkling Wine)
Maculan Torcolato (Italian Dessert Wine)

HOLIDAY ROAST

Don't wait for a holiday to serve this delicious brisket.

    2 5-ounce packages mixed dried fruit
    1 4-pound brisket
    1 tablespoon oil
  1/4 teaspoon salt
  1/4 teaspoon pepper
  1/4 teaspoon garlic powder
    1 cup Concord grape wine
    1 medium carrot, finely chopped
    1 large onion, finely chopped
    1 large orange, peeled and sectioned
    1 large apple, cored and sliced
    1 teaspoon cinnamon
  1/2 teaspoon ginger
    3 tablespoons flour

Soak the dried fruit overnight in water to cover and save liquid. Brown meat in oil in a heavy pan with tight-fitting lid. Add salt, pepper, garlic powder, wine, carrot, onion and any liquid from fruit. Bring to a boil, cover, reduce heat and simmer 2 1/2 hours or until tender. Add all fruit, cinnamon and ginger. Cook 15 minutes. Remove brisket and keep warm.

Sprinkle flour over pan juices, raise heat, and stir constantly until gravy thickens. *Serves 8.*

 This recipe serves 16, when you offer the recommended 3-ounce size portions of meat, and fat and cholesterol are reduced. Choose leaner cuts of meat such as round and sirloin for the roast. Carrots are a great addition, and add anti-oxidant vitamin A.

 Ridge Zinfandel (California Red)
Mt. Veeder Cabernet Sauvignon (California Red)

PECAN PIE

We're nuts over this sweet dessert.

  1/4 cup butter
  1/2 cup sugar
    1 cup light corn syrup
    3 eggs
       Dash of salt
    1 cup chopped pecans
    1 unbaked 9-inch deep-dish pie shell

Cream butter and sugar together in mixer until fluffy. Add syrup and beat well. Add eggs, one at a time. Add salt and pecans. Pour into pie shell and bake at 325 degrees for 40 minutes. *Serves 6 to 8.*

 This dessert is very rich in folic acid, an important B vitamin used in making red blood cells. Nuts are packed with nutrients and fiber, but still high in fat. Use margarine instead of butter, and 3/4 cup egg substitute to change this recipe from high cholesterol to no cholesterol.

KING RANCH CASSEROLE

You don't have to be a king to feast on this one. This delicious Texas casserole doesn't cost a king's ransom to prepare, and feeds a large group.

10 corn tortillas
 1 3 to 4-pound chicken, boiled, deboned and torn into strips
 1 10 3/4-ounce can mushroom soup
 1 10 3/4-ounce can chicken soup
2/3 cup chicken broth
 1 onion, chopped
 1 10-ounce can Ro-tel tomatoes
 8 ounces grated cheddar cheese

In a greased 9x13-inch baking dish, layer half of all the ingredients. Repeat, ending with cheese. Bake at 300 degrees for 1 hour. *Serves 8 to 10.*

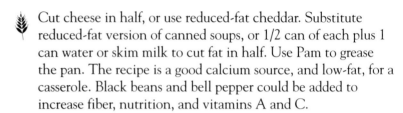 Cut cheese in half, or use reduced-fat cheddar. Substitute reduced-fat version of canned soups, or 1/2 can of each plus 1 can water or skim milk to cut fat in half. Use Pam to grease the pan. The recipe is a good calcium source, and low-fat, for a casserole. Black beans and bell pepper could be added to increase fiber, nutrition, and vitamins A and C.

Iron Horse Chardonnay (California White)
R. H. Phillips Sauvignon Blanc (California White)

TWO-MINUTE MICROWAVE FUDGE

This fudge is easy to make and tastes like Mom's old-fashioned fudge, but without the mess. Use 2 tablespoons milk and 2 tablespoons Rum for a special flavor.

 1 pound confectioners' sugar
1/2 cup cocoa powder
1/4 cup milk
1/2 cup butter
 1 teaspoon vanilla
1/2 cup nuts (optional)

Blend together sugar and cocoa in a microwave-safe dish. Pour in milk. Place butter on top of mixture. Heat 2 minutes in microwave on high. Stir well. Add vanilla and nuts, stirring well until blended. Chill in an 8x8x2-inch glass dish until set. Cut and enjoy. *Yields 32 pieces.*

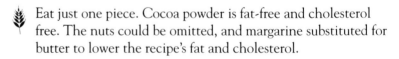 Eat just one piece. Cocoa powder is fat-free and cholesterol free. The nuts could be omitted, and margarine substituted for butter to lower the recipe's fat and cholesterol.

Gruet Blanc de Noir (New Mexico Sparkling Wine)
S. Anderson Brut (California Sparkling Wine)

WILD MUSHROOM SOUP

ORZO PASTA
with Vegetable Tomato Sauce

BLACK BEAN PIZZA

CHOCOLATE CHOCOLATE CHIP CAKE

TEXAS LAMB STEW

Everything is better in the beautiful surroundings of the Kimbell Art Museum. The award-winning Louis Kahn design of the building generates a cosmopolitan air suitable for the masterpieces it holds.

Come nourish the body and soul at the Kimbell Buffet, where international visitors and locals meet. The buffet has greatly expanded its collection since 1981, when Buffet Manager Shelby Schafer began developing meals for museum-goers.

Schafer welcomed the challenge. She plans popular menus and seasonal and holiday dishes for everything from 1,000-member galas to light lunches on the patio. She hired an enthusiastic staff. "I can train them to cook our food," Schafer says, "but I can't train them to be friendly. That has to come naturally."

Kimbell Art Museum
——The Buffet Restaurant——

Among the Kimbell offerings are Autumn Celebration, and Green Chiles and Rice soups, and Pasta and Pesto Salad, the Kimbell Club, wines and beer, espresso and cappuccino. Light entrees are served on Saturday evenings. Applesauce Cake, Lemon Cream Cheese Pie and Peach Bread Pudding are among the desserts that please art patrons' palates.

Schafer enjoys expanding her horizons for the Saturday evening dinners, which feature music and wine tastings. "Some of our best dishes have been made from what is on hand," she said. "Our most recent creation was Kimbell Lasagna, made from caponata (eggplant relish), shrimp, and sun-dried tomato pesto."

In keeping with the latest food trends, Schafer is health-conscious. In soups, she is using milk instead of cream, and vegetables as thickeners. "Today our customers are interested in different combinations of ingredients," she says. "Ten years ago we would have never put fruit in salads or on sandwiches."

Schafer relies on her own cookbook, "The Kimbell Cookbook," for menu ideas. "When I need a good salad, sauce or soup, I turn to recipes from The French Apron School of Cooking and Cuisine Concepts." Schafer has been a student of the school since 1979. The result is that the Kimbell Buffet staff teasingly calls her the "Curator of Culinary Arts."

──────────── LIGHTER BITES ────────────

Choose a clear soup, a crunchy salad with vinaigrette dressing, any steamed, baked or broiled entree without rich sauce or cheese, and fruit salad for dessert.

The Kimbell Art Museum
3333 Camp Bowie Blvd.
Fort Worth, TX 76107
817/332-8451

WILD MUSHROOM SOUP

Wild mushrooms are widely available, either fresh or dried, in local markets.

>   5 cups chicken stock (divided use)
> 1 1/2 ounces dried porcini
>   1 teaspoon light olive oil
>   1 medium onion, chopped
>   1 stalk celery, chopped
>   1 carrot, chopped
>   4 cloves garlic, minced
>   3/4 cup sherry
>   1/2 pound mushrooms, chopped
>   6 ounce package brown and wild rice
>   9 ounces frozen chopped spinach
>   1/2 cup cream or milk (optional)
>   1/3 teaspoon pepper

Bring 1 cup of chicken stock to a boil and add dried mushrooms to soak for half an hour. Strain, saving liquid. Rinse mushrooms well, removing any sand. Chop them. Strain the liquid through fine cheesecloth and set aside. In a large sauce pan, heat oil and sauté onion, celery, carrot and garlic until tender, stirring occasionally.

Stir in sherry and reduce by half. Add remaining stock, wild mushrooms and soaking liquid, mushrooms and rice and simmer for 20-30 minutes. Add spinach and cream or milk at the last and heat through. Add pepper and salt if desired. *Serves 4.*

 Sauté with Pam. Substitute skim milk or omit altogether.

 Buena Vista Pinot Noir (California Red)
Chateau La Tonnell (French Red)

ORZO PASTA *with Vegetable Tomato Sauce*

Another small pasta may be substituted.

>   8 ounces orzo
>   1 cup chopped red onion
>   1 teaspoon light olive oil
>   8 mushrooms, chopped
>   4 cloves garlic, minced
>   1/2 cup red wine
>   14 1/2-ounce can tomatoes, drained
>   2 tablespoons sun-dried tomatoes
>   3 tablespoons tomato paste
>   1 each red, yellow roasted bell peppers
>   2 tablespoons chopped fresh basil
>   1/4 teaspoon red pepper flakes
>   1/2 teaspoon anchovy paste

Cook pasta. Drain well and toss with drops of oil and set aside. Sauté onion until tender. Add mushrooms and garlic and sauté for 10 minutes. Add wine and reduce to half. Pour in minced sun-dried tomatoes, chopped canned tomatoes and tomato paste, and simmer 30 minutes until thick. Peel and dice peppers and add remaining ingredients. Taste for seasoning. *Serves 4-6.*

 Mondavi Carneros Chardonnay (California White)
Duboeuf Beaujolais-Villages (French Red)

BLACK BEAN PIZZA

A vegetarian calorie-counter's delight.

- 1 pound dried black beans
- 1 cup chopped onion
- 4 garlic cloves, minced
- 1 poblano pepper, peeled and diced
- 8 corn tortillas or pita bread rounds
- 1 1/2 cups grated Monterey Jack cheese
- 1/2 cup light sour cream

SALSA
- 1/4 cup minced onion
- 1 each red and yellow bell pepper, roasted, peeled and diced
- 1 jalapeno pepper, seeded and minced
- 1 1/2 cups fresh seeded and diced tomato
- 2 tablespoons minced cilantro
- 2 tablespoons lime juice

Pick over and rinse beans. Place in saucepan with 4 cups water. Bring to a boil, cover and remove from heat for 1 hour. Drain off soaking water and add 4 cups water and remaining ingredients. Simmer 1 hour, or until tender. Mash beans, adding water if necessary. Season to taste. To make the salsa, mix all ingredients and chill.

To assemble, spread tortilla or pita with beans, salsa, and cheese. Bake until hot, then place a dollop of sour cream on each pizza. *Serves 8.*

 Beans are rich in nutrition, fat free, and contain soluble fiber which can lower cholesterol.

 Fetzer Barrel Fermented Chardonnay (California White)
Oberhellmann Cabernet Sauvignon (Texas Red)

CHOCOLATE CHOCOLATE CHIP CAKE

Shafer says, "Dessert must be chocolate."

- 1 cup butter
- 1/2 cup shortening
- 3 cups sugar
- 5 eggs
- 3 cups flour
- 1/2 cup cocoa
- 1/2 teaspoon each baking powder, salt
- 1 cup milk
- 2 tablespoons vanilla
- 1 cup chocolate chips

Grease and flour a Bundt cake pan. Cream butter, shortening and sugar. Add eggs, one at a time, mixing well. Combine dry ingredients. Stir half of mixture into sugar mixture. Alternate with half of the milk and remaining dry ingredients. Add vanilla, chocolate chips, and stir well. Pour into prepared pan and bake at 325 for 1 hour. Cool 10 minutes before turning out of pan. *Serves 12.*

 Grease pan with Pam. Use 1/2 cup margarine for butter and shortening, 10 egg whites for whole eggs and skim milk.

 Roederer Estates Brut (California Sparkling Wine)
Chateau Rayne Vigneau (French Dessert Wine)

TEXAS LAMB STEW

*This spicy stew is not for the faint at heart.
Beef or venison may be substituted, but the
stew will not be the same.*

5	tablespoons peanut oil (divided use)
7	ancho chiles
4	pounds boneless lamb shoulder, trimmed, cubed, and patted dry
2	cups chopped onion
1 1/2	cups chopped carrots
6	garlic cloves, minced
2	cups chopped red bell peppers
7	cups lamb or chicken stock
3/4	cup pecan pieces
1	cup hulled pumpkin seeds
3	cups tomatoes, peeled, seeded and chopped
2	cups fresh pineapple, cut in chunks
3/4	teaspoon ground cumin
	Salt
1/4	teaspoon cayenne
	Cinnamon

Sauté chiles in 2 tablespoons peanut oil over medium heat for 2 to 3 minutes. Do not overcook or they will turn bitter. Drop into a saucepan of boiling water and simmer for 10 minutes. Drain and cool.

In a large stew pot, sauté lamb in 1 1/2 tablespoons peanut oil until it is evenly browned. Add onions, carrots, garlic, red pepper and 6 cups of the stock. Simmer over medium-low heat for 15 minutes.

Remove stem and seeds from peppers. Sauté pecans and pumpkin seeds in 1 1/2 tablespoons peanut oil until they begin to brown. Combine chiles, pecans, pumpkin seeds and remaining 1 cup of stock. Puree in a processor to make a paste. Add all or part of the paste (depending on the heat desired) to lamb and vegetables along with tomatoes, pineapple, cumin. Simmer slowly for another 45 minutes to an hour. Add salt, cayenne and cinnamon to taste. *Serves 12.*

 Use 3 pounds lamb and sauté with just 1 1/2 teaspoons oil. Cut nuts and seeds to 1/3 cup total, and sauté with Pam. Recipe is high in fiber, vitamins A and B, and minerals.

 Pheasant Ridge Cabernet Sauvignon (Texas Red)
Masi Amarone (Italian Red)

FLAN AUX CHAMPIGNONS

FRUIT TABOULE

ZUCCHINI FLAN
with Garlic Cream

POULET AU VINAIGRE

SOUFFLÉ CITRON

Bonjour! Friendly smiles beam above crisp French bakers' coats to greet patrons of la Madeleine French Bakery and Café. There is nothing else like it.

French-born Patrick Esquerré (ess-kerry) has pioneered authentic French bread-making in Texas. La Madeleine has introduced the wonderful taste and texture of the fresh breads of France to legions of Fort Worth and Arlington locals who were raised on store-bought white bread.

To complement the array of breads and pastries available at la Madeleine, Esquerré added breakfast items, soups (including classic French onion), salads (Caesar, spinach, wild field greens, tuna Niçoise, and fruit), cold and hot sandwiches such as croque monsieurs, quiches, pizzas, and pastas. The tantalizing aroma of rosemary roasted chickens on the rotisserie mingles with the scent of freshly baked bread, driving customers to new heights of hunger and anticipation.

Esquerré fostered his love of deliciously prepared fresh food during his childhood in his native chateau country of France. "We grew everything on our farm, from chicken to beef to strawberries and green beans," he says. "Everything was fresh, natural and organic. Each meal was a real event, with the whole family gathered together."

A cookbook containing a collection of the recipes Esquerré remembers most fondly from his childhood is available for patrons who would like to recreate the taste of the chateau country in their homes.

Esquerré's love of his business is eclipsed only by his passion for roses — he has 100 rose bushes at his home. Antiques are his other love; his ideal vacation is cruising through France, stopping along the way to seek out the beauty of the past.

La Madeleine has that distinctive French beauty. The rich wood paneling, mingled with brick and stone, brings warmth to the restaurant's interior. Sunshine beams down on the Fort Worth restaurant year round. And patrons may enjoy the brisk breezy winters and hot sultry summers at outdoor trestle tables. Bon appétit!

LIGHTER BITES

Whole Wheat and 7-Grain bread are fat-free and high in fiber. Choose a ham, turkey or roast beef sandwich, with lettuce, tomato and Dijon mustard, the Rotisserie Chicken or Plat du Jour. Have fruit or a green salad with just 1 tablespoon dressing, instead of Caesar Salad.

6140 Camp Bowie Blvd.
Fort Worth, TX 76116
817/732-4655

2101 North Collins Street
Arlington, TX 76011
817/459-1327

FLAN AUX CHAMPIGNONS

This tart is a favorite from Esquerré's childhood.

2 1/4 cups milk
  6 eggs
    Salt and white pepper to taste
    Nutmeg, to taste
    Butter for cake pan
  9 large mushrooms
    Vinegar or lemon juice
2 1/2 tablespoons unsalted butter
    Chopped chives for garnish

Heat milk just until boiling. Beat eggs with a fork, adding salt, pepper and nutmeg, and add milk. Butter an 8 or 9-inch round cake pan. Pour in mixture. Bake tart for 30 minutes in a preheated 400 degree oven, setting pan in a roasting pan filled 3/4 full with water.

Wash mushrooms in water containing a small amount of vinegar or lemon juice. Dry and slice. Cook mushrooms in butter and add chives, salt and pepper. Cook about 10 minutes. Top unmolded tart with mushrooms and chives. *Serves 4.*

 Substitute skim milk and 1 1/2 cups Egg Beaters; sauté mushrooms in 1 teaspoon margarine, and spray pan with Pam to reduce to 1 gram fat per serving.

 Mondavi Carneros Pinot Noir (California Red)
Jekel Cabernet Franc (California Red)

FRUIT TABOULE

Surprise your guests with this unique and nutritious dessert.

  1 cup water
1/2 cup white wine
1/2 cup sugar
  2 tea bags
  5 mint leaves
  1 cup semolina couscous
  3 cups assorted diced fruit in season
  5 mint leaves for garnish

Mix water, white wine, sugar, tea and mint. Bring to a boil, strain, and then pour over the couscous. Mix, allow to swell, and fluff with a fork. Fold the fruit into the couscous and mix gently. Garnish with mint leaves. *Serves 6.*

 This is a great recipe for a non-fat dessert!

 Chateau De Baun Symphony (California Dessert Wine)
Chateau Doisy Daene (French Dessert Wine)

ZUCCHINI FLAN *with Garlic Cream Sauce*

The garlic cream sauce is also wonderful with chicken or veal.

1 3/4 pounds zucchini
4 eggs
2 cups cream (divided use)
3 sticks butter
2 cloves garlic
Juice of 2 lemons
Lettuce leaves for garnish
Parsley sprigs for garnish
Salt and pepper

Cut washed zucchini into large pieces and steam for 20 minutes. Puree. Add eggs one by one, then half the cream and season. Butter small molds, or a soufflé dish. Fill with mixture and place in a hot water bath in a 400-degree oven for 20 to 30 minutes. Flan will be done when a metal skewer comes out clean and hot.

To prepare sauce, cook the unpeeled garlic for 10 minutes in salted water. Peel and puree. Add remainder of cream. When boiling point is reached, remove from heat and add small chunks of butter while stirring constantly to thicken sauce. Season and add lemon juice to mixture.

Unmold the zucchini flan in center of platter. Garnish with lettuce leaves. Decorate flan with sprigs of parsley. Surround with semi-warm sauce and serve. *Serves 6.*

 Substitute Egg Beaters, evaporated skim milk, and 1/4 cup margarine. Use Pam on molds. Modified recipe has as much calcium as 1 glass of milk.

 Geyser Peak Semchard (California White)
Kendall-Jackson Pinot Noir (California Red)

POULET AU VINAIGRE

Add green salad and potatoes to complete a country French meal.

2 chickens, cut into pieces
  Unsalted butter
2 cloves garlic, unpeeled
4 tablespoons Dijon mustard
4 tablespoons tomato paste
5 tablespoons white wine
5 tablespoons wine vinegar
1/2 cup crème fraîche (optional)
2 tablespoons Worcestershire sauce

In a sauté pan, brown chicken in butter. Add garlic and simmer covered for 20 minutes without adding additional liquid. Degrease the pan juices. Whisk together mustard, tomato paste and white wine. Add to chicken and cook an additional 25 minutes.

Reduce vinegar to 2 tablespoons. Baste chicken with vinegar and add crème fraîche and Worcestershire sauce. Remove chicken, discarding garlic, and arrange on platter. Add sauce. *Serves 6 to 8.*

 To significantly lower fat and cholesterol, sauté chicken with 1 tablespoon margarine and remove skin before serving.

 Preston Viognier (California White)
Paul Jaboulet Gigondas (French Red)

SOUFFLÉ CITRON

This soufflé is a quick and elegant treat for late-night guests.

4 large lemons
4 eggs, separated
1/4 cup powdered sugar
1 tablespoon lemon juice
  Juice of 1 orange
1 teaspoon Grand Marnier (optional)

Cut off 1/2 inch tip of each lemon. Remove pulp. The empty lemons will serve as soufflé molds. Cut a small slice off the bottoms so they will stand. Mix yolks and sugar together in bowl until creamy. Add the juices and Grand Marnier.

Beat egg whites to just stiff peaks, and fold into mixture. Fill each lemon and bake in preheated 375 degree oven 10 minutes. Sprinkle with powdered sugar and serve immediately. *Serves 4.*

 Roederer Brut (French Champagne)
Chateau Raymond-Lafon (French Dessert Wine)
Domaine Carneros (California Sparkling Wine)

MISTO MARE PIAZZA

LUMACHE BELLAVISTA

COSTATA DI VITELLO ALLA MILANESE

SCALOPPINE ALLA GENOVESE

INSALATA DI PESCE

Ristorante

LA PIAZZA

Buona sera! Vito Ciraci, an Italian gentleman as polished as the marble beneath his feet, greets patrons at the door of his posh La Piazza on Seventh Street. Slip into one of the sixty seats of this intimate restaurant, and enjoy Italian food at its finest. The classical music and soft murmur of conversation at other tables is broken only by the arrival of another of the chef's creations.

The menu offers a bounty of Italian delicacies, from Carpaccio Alla Toscana and Scampi Alla Napoletana, to traditional soups and salads, pastas, seafood and meats. The kitchen is not bound by its printed menu, and will accommodate unique requests. Ciraci notes that, in the evening, eighty percent of the orders are not from the menu. "That is why I have a small restaurant," he says with a smile.

Connoisseurs of all things Italian will enjoy La Piazza. "I am trying to introduce people to what Italy is all about," says Ciraci. Chef Salvo Pampallona is a native of Sicily, and spent many years in Milan before christening La Piazza's kitchen. The authenticity of his cuisine is evident in dishes such as Risotto Alla Pescatora and Veal Chop with Mushrooms.

Ciraci is an advocate of the Mediterranean regional diet. "We can make meals with no fat," he says. An example is the signature dish Penne All' Arrabbiata, pasta with a spicy tomato sauce. "My olive oil has no cholesterol. Add a glass of wine, and your health will be good."

Guests are invited to linger leisurely over dinner and dessert. Superb service and selective wine offerings complete the experience. "Our wine list is predominantly Italian," says Ciraci. In addition, a collection of limited edition wine is available from the "special" wine list.

Ciraci is a man without relaxation. He is the consummate host, and personally oversees his patrons' enjoyment. La Piazza is his second home, and his family is often there. Their genuine Italian style punctuates the restaurant with flair and the pleasures of Italy.

LIGHTER BITES

Enjoy Tortellini In Brodo, or Insalate Con Gamberetti, Radicchio Grigliato, or Insalata Della Casa with dressings on the side. Choose Triglia Alla "Livornese" or Scaloppine Al Marsala for dinner.

3431 West Seventh Street
Fort Worth, TX 76107
817/334-0000

MISTO MARE PIAZZA

*This special dish is a creation of the Ciracis for
their restaurant.*

1/4 cup olive oil
1/2 pound calamari
  8 large shrimp, peeled and deveined
1/2 pound scallops
  1 teaspoon chopped garlic
1/8 teaspoon red pepper
   Dry white wine
  3 tomatoes, diced
  8 fresh basil leaves, chopped
1/4 cup butter
  1 cup chicken bouillon
  6 cups cooked linguine or rice

Heat skillet with olive oil over medium heat. When hot, add calamari, shrimp and scallops. Sauté for 2 to 3 minutes. Drain juices from pan. Add garlic, red pepper, and splash with wine. Salt and pepper to taste. Add chopped tomatoes, basil, butter and chicken bouillon. Heat for 2 to 3 more minutes and serve with linguine or rice. *Serves 4.*

 This is a healthy, low-fat seafood meal. Sauté with 1 tablespoon olive oil, and use 1 tablespoon margarine to replace butter.

 Giacosa Arneis (Italian White)
Teruzzi & Puthod Vernaccia di San Gimignano (Italian White)

LUMACHE BELLAVISTA *(Snails Bellevue)*

*The name of this dish means "good looking"
and it is true.*

12 escargot
  1 tablespoon butter
1/2 teaspoon minced garlic
   Dry white wine
  1 tomato, chopped
   Salt and pepper
   Red pepper flakes
   Brandy
  1 tablespoon chopped fresh basil

Cook escargot over medium heat for approximately 2 minutes. Add butter and garlic. Simmer briefly. Sprinkle with dry white wine, add tomato, salt and pepper to taste and a pinch of red pepper.

Splash with brandy and add chopped basil. Serve immediately. *Serves 2.*

 Escargot is fat-free. Substitute 1/2 tablespoon margarine for butter.

 Pio Cesare Barbera d'Alba (Italian Red)
Taurino Salice Salentino (Italian Red)

Costata Di Vitello Alla Milanese *(Veal Chop Milanese)*

Milanese is a classic preparation of bone-in veal with flour, egg, breadcrumbs and Parmesan.

16-ounce veal chop
 4 eggs
 2 tablespoons chopped Italian parsley
1/4 cup Parmesan cheese
   Salt and pepper
 1 cup fine bread crumbs
1/4 cup soybean oil
   Arugula and lemon, for garnish

Place veal chop between two sheets of plastic wrap on a cutting board and pound, without hitting the bone, into a 1/4-inch thick circle. Beat eggs, and add salt and pepper, Italian parsley and Parmesan cheese. Place veal in bread crumbs and coat evenly. Place veal in egg mixture and coat both sides. Repeat procedure until veal chop is well-coated on both sides.

Heat oil in skillet and cook veal approximately 35 to 40 seconds per side. Garnish with lemon and arugula. *Serves 2.*

 Veal is a lean choice for quality protein. Substitute Egg Beaters, and bake chops or use Pam to sauté.

 Castello Vicchiomaggio Chianti Classico (Italian Red)
Castello di Gabbiano Ania (Italian Red)

Scaloppine Alla Genovese

This recipe is the creation of La Piazza's chef, Salvo Pampallona.

1/4 cup soybean oil
 6 slices veal scaloppine
   Flour
1/4 cup sparkling white wine
 8 fresh asparagus spears
   Salt and pepper
 4 slices mozzarella cheese
1/4 cup heavy cream

Heat oil in a sauté pan. Dust scaloppine in flour and place in hot pan. Cook both sides until light brown. Place on paper towels to drain excess oil. Pour remaining oil out of pan and discard.

Off heat, return scaloppine to pan, splash with sparkling wine, and top with asparagus spears. Salt and pepper to taste. Add mozzarella slices, cover with heavy cream and cook until sauce thickens. Place pan under broiler until cheese and cream start to brown. *Serves 2.*

 Use only 1 teaspoon oil, and substitute evaporated skim milk and 1 ounce of grated, reduced-fat cheese.

 Renato Ratti Dolcetto d'Alba (Italian Red)
Banfi Centine Rose di Montalcino (Italian Red)

INSALATA DI PESCE

Regular octopus instead of Portuguese can be used in this specialty from the south of Italy. Octopus and calamari are usually purchased frozen.

  1 pound shrimp
  4 quarts water
  2 tablespoons black pepper
  6 bay leaves
    Nutmeg
  1 pound mussels, steamed and
    removed from shells
  1 pound scallops, boiled
    for 2 to 3 minutes
  2 pounds calamari, cleaned,
    sliced into rings, and
    boiled 10 to 15 minutes
  2 pounds Portuguese octopus
  1 bunch celery, chopped
  1 red bell pepper, chopped
  1 yellow bell pepper, chopped
1/2 cup Italian parsley, chopped
  1 cup large capers
    Salt and pepper
    Juice of 7 lemons
  3 quarts olive oil (divided use)

GARNISH
  2 heads radicchio
  6 tomatoes, quartered
    Italian parsley, chopped

To cook shrimp, bring 4 quarts of water to boil with black pepper, bay leaves and nutmeg. Add shrimp and cook until pink, approximately 2 to 3 minutes. Drain, saving shrimp water. Remove shells and set shrimp aside. Return the shrimp water to a boil. Cook mussels, scallops, then calamari and set aside to cool. Dip the octopus in this boiling water 2 or 3 times until tentacles are straight. Place the entire octopus in the water and cook for 1 hour, or until a fork slides in easily. Chop into 3/4-inch pieces.

Allow all the seafood to cool for 1 hour after it is cooked. Then place the seafood in a large mixing bowl, add celery, peppers, parsley and mix together. Add capers and salt and pepper to taste.

Pour lemon juice over seafood mixture. Mix thoroughly with 1/4 cup olive oil. Place in a glass bowl and pour remaining olive oil over mixture. Chill for 2 to 3 hours.

To serve, make a bowl with 3 leaves of radicchio. Place drained salad inside the leaves, sprinkle with parsley, and garnish with 3 tomato quarters. *Serves 8.*

 Use just 1/4 cup oil in dressing, and omit remaining oil.

 Ceretto Blange (Italian White)
Santa Margherita Pinot Grigio (Italian White)

FACING PAGE
Rotisserie Rendezvous
*Paul Willis, left, Georgia Kostas,
Michel Baudouin, Deborah Moncrief, Vito Ciraci.*

FOLLOWING PAGE
Days of Wine and Roses
*Michael Thomson, left, John Kennedy,
Wes Glover, Walter Kaufmann.*

AFRICAN QUEEN
POTATO AU GRATIN DAUPHINOIS
LA DAURADE AU FOUR
VINAIGRETTE DE LA MAMAN TONIA
POT AU FEU D'AGNEAU

Michel Baudouin has made an art of adapting French cuisine to local tastes. He describes the fare at Le Chardonnay as "French Continental with a Texas accent."

Baudouin (boo-dwon) has an outgoing personality and refuses to take himself too seriously. His culinary philosophy is reflected in the cheerful ambiance and the fresh, innovative and attractive dishes at Le Chardonnay.

In France, Le Chardonnay would be considered a brasserie, the French hybrid of a bistro and restaurant. The food is akin to bistro fare, with pâté, onion tart and french fries, yet the airy openness and white tablecloths connote a formal restaurant. This eclectic setting is enhanced by the patio, with its umbrella-shaded tables, next to Baudouin's lush herb garden.

Spacious indoor dining rooms with huge windows and fresh flowers establish a tranquil mood. Baudouin says, "People used to go to a restaurant for a food experience. Now dining out is the evening's entertainment." Diners savor Le Chardonnay's trademark dishes, from succulent Lamb Chops with Goat Cheese to the Cassoulet of Fish with Jalapeño Béarnaise. Le Chardonnay boasts the best-dressed dessert menu in town, with more than a dozen choices.

Le Chardonnay lives up to its viniferous name. Staff members are well-versed in the exceptional wine list and the 27 choices of wines by the glass. If in doubt, consult the menu. It is color-coded to indicate the varietal which best complements each dish.

To enhance customers' appreciation for French fare, Baudouin offers a wine and food matching dinner series. Each features three courses with accompanying wines.

A new rotisserie and a carry-out window in the bar make Le Chardonnay's food accessible to busy, hungry people. "A certain amount of the population have kids. With basketball, soccer and cheerleading they can't cook because of shuttling children all over the place," says Baudouin with a grin. "We're just making quality food available to those people — they really deserve it."

LIGHTER BITES

Select Black Bean Soup, Moules Marinière, Salade Michel, Turkey Scaloppine Grenobloise, Seafood Fettucine Primavera, or Cote D'Agneau Montrachet grilled without butter.

2443 Forest Park Blvd.
Fort Worth, TX 76110
817/926-5622

AFRICAN QUEEN

Baudouin's own creation has become a Le Chardonnay classic.

2 bananas
16 sheets phyllo pastry
Melted butter

CARAMEL SAUCE
2 tablespoons sugar
1 teaspoon water
1 teaspoon vanilla
2 cups heavy cream

GARNISH
4 large strawberries
20 orange wedges
4 mint leaves
4 scoops vanilla ice cream

Cook sugar and water in heavy saucepan over low heat until mixture turns a rich golden color. In another saucepan, bring cream and vanilla to a boil. Add to sugar and cook, stirring constantly with a whisk, until smooth. Let cool.

Peel bananas and cut in half lengthwise. Brush one sheet phyllo with melted butter. Sprinkle with sugar. Repeat 3 times, stacking the sheets. Wrap one banana half in the pastry, refrigerate, and repeat with remaining banana halves. Bake wrapped bananas on sheet pan in pre-heated 375-degree oven until golden and crisp. To serve, place caramel sauce on half of each plate. Decorate the other half with fruit garnishes. Place cooked banana on sauce and top with ice cream. Serve immediately. *Serves 4.*

 Spray butter-flavor Pam on pastry sheets, and substitute evaporated skim milk and low-fat ice cream.

 Paul Jaboulet Beaumes-de-Venice (French Dessert Wine)
Maison Deutz Brut (California Sparkling Wine)

POTATO AU GRATIN DAUPHINOIS

This classic potato dish is good with red meat, poultry or fish.

4 large Idaho potatoes
3 cloves garlic, minced
1 pint heavy cream
1/2 cup grated Jarlsberg cheese
1 tablespoon butter
1/2 teaspoon grated nutmeg
Salt and pepper to taste

Peel potatoes and slice thin. Mix cream, nutmeg, salt, pepper and cheese, and toss with potato slices. Butter a 9x14-inch baking dish. Sprinkle with garlic. Using a slotted spoon, arrange potatoes evenly in baking dish. Pour in remaining cream and bake at 375 degrees for 1 hour until golden brown. *Serves 4.*

 Substitute evaporated skim milk and spray baking dish with Pam to sharply reduce calories, fat and cholesterol.

 Stonestreet Pinot Noir (California Red)
Prunotto Occhetti Nebbiolo d'Alba (Italian Red)

LA DAURADE AU FOUR (*Baked Snapper Mediterranean*)

This fish dish does not have to be cooked at the last minute.

- 4 6-ounce red snapper or halibut fillets
- 4 large ripe tomatoes
- 1 lemon
- 2 shallots
- 1/2 rib celery
- 4 fresh basil leaves
- 4 small sprigs parsley
- 2 bay leaves
- 1 sprig fresh thyme
- 8 black peppercorns
- 2 tablespoons olive oil
- 2 cups Sauvignon Blanc
- 3/4 cup water

Peel, seed and chop tomatoes. Slice lemon, shallot and celery. Wrap basil, parsley, bay leaves, thyme and peppercorns in cheesecloth to make a bouquet garni. Place tomatoes, lemon, shallot and celery evenly across the bottom of a 9x13-inch baking dish. Lightly salt and pepper fish and place side by side on vegetables. Add wine and water to cover vegetables and half of the fish. Press bouquet garni into the liquid. Cover with foil and bake in a preheated 400-degree oven for 20 minutes.

To serve, discard bouquet garni, and place fish on a serving platter. Reduce broth, adjust seasoning, and pass separately as a sauce. Serve with pasta or asparagus. *Serves 4.*

 Houtz Sauvignon Blanc (California White)
Moreau Chablis (French White)

VINAIGRETTE DE LA MAMAN TONIA

Tonia, Baudouin's foster mother, made this dressing every Sunday for her wonderful brunch on the farm where he grew up.

- 1 tablespoon Dijon mustard
- 2 tablespoons red wine vinegar
- 2 tablespoons vegetable oil
- 2 tablespoons olive oil
- 1 soft-boiled egg, chilled
  Salt and pepper to taste

Whisk together mustard, salt, pepper and vinegar. Drizzle oil in a thin stream, whisking to emulsify. Peel egg and add to vinaigrette. Crush with a fork and stir. Toss with soft lettuces torn into bite-size pieces. Serve immediately. *Serves 4.*

 Use just 1 tablespoon each of vegetable and olive oil, and substitute 2 cooked egg whites for soft-boiled egg.

 Cuvaison Chardonnay (California White)
Bonny Doon Clos de Gilroy (California Red)

POT AU FEU D'AGNEAU

"Use a good wine for this dish," Baudouin *says. "If wine is not good to drink, it is not good to cook with."*

- 4 **lamb shanks**
- 8 **medium new potatoes**
- 2 **carrots, cut into 1-inch pieces**
- 1 **turnip, quartered**
- 4 **leeks, white part only**
- 2 **whole garlic cloves**
- 8 **fresh pearl onions**
- 2 **bay leaves**
- 1 **sprig fresh thyme**
- 8 **whole black peppercorns**
- 1/2 **bottle white wine**
- 1 **teaspoon salt**
  Puff pastry sheets
- 1 **egg, lightly beaten**

GARNISH
Dijon mustard
Sea salt
Cornichons

Prepare vegetables. Preheat oven to 350 degrees. Select a large pot tall enough to stand up lamb shanks and fit in oven. Place shanks in center of pot and surround with vegetables and garlic. Wrap bay leaves, thyme and peppercorns in a small piece of cheesecloth. Add to pot with wine, salt, and enough water to cover two-thirds of the shanks.

Bring to a boil, and skim off foam. Seal the stock pot's lid to its rim with puff pastry by lining the inside rim, placing lid on pot, and folding dough edges up over lid. Brush dough with egg wash.

Bring pot contents to a boil on the stove. Transfer to preheated oven and bake for 1 1/2 hours. To serve, bring unopened pot to table, cut the pastry seal with a knife and open. The fragrance will fill the room.

Serve the shanks in a large soup bowl, add vegetables, and ladle stock on top. Pass garnish. *Serves 4.*

 To reduce calories by half, use phyllo dough for puff pasrty, sprayed with butter-flavor Pam, and 2 egg whites for egg.

 Stags' Leap Cabernet Sauvignon (California Red)
Beaucastel Chateauneuf-de-Pape (French Red)

LUCILE'S MEAT LOAF
with Tomato Sauce

CRAB CAKES
with Roasted Garlic Sauce

EMERALD COAST FISHERMAN'S STEW

Beyond your wildest dreams of culinary success — there is Lucile's. This runaway Fort Worth favorite opened in April 1993, and chef Paul Willis hasn't slept since. No wonder; the American classic food at Lucile's is second to none.

Robert McLean founded the restaurant and named it after his mother. He is compiling a cookbook, "Traditions," of treasured recipes from his family and the great home cooks of the South. Lucile's is steeped in Fort Worth restaurant tradition. Its building, completed in 1927, has housed the legendary Steve's, Finley's Cafeteria, and the Black-Eyed Pea.

Willis has revived Southern favorites. The Fried Green Tomatoes appetizer kicks off a great Maryland Crab Cakes dinner. Top that off with Crème Brûleé, wash it down with Café Latte, and you have been around the gastronomic world in four courses. For those who prefer a lighter meal, the Wilted Spinach Salad with Hot Bacon Dressing is a wonderful throwback to the past. Lucile's menu honors tradition with its Hickory House-smoked Ham, reflecting fond memories of Steve's famous ham sandwiches, and desserts from Finley's era ("We can't make them fast enough," says Willis). Daily blue plate and blackboard specials draw droves of diners.

Willis was born near the north end of the Chisholm Trail in Kansas City and moved with his family to The Netherlands in 1978. He attended the University of Texas at Arlington and Florida State before coming to Fort Worth as chef of The River House. Willis then trained at the Culinary Institute of America, and was completing an internship in Dallas when McLean asked him to return to Fort Worth. "Attending the CIA was a dream come true," says this down-to-earth chef. "You have to love this business. I like the hours and the pressure, because it tests my performance."

Perform he does, but only in the kitchen. "I would be a musician, but I'm terrible." It's good he stays in his element: Fort Worth needed a Lucile's with a chef like Willis.

Lucile's
A STATESIDE BISTRO

LIGHTER BITES

Have Jumbo Shrimp or Greek Salad with dressing on the side (omit peppers). Choose a Pizza without olives, peperoncini or sausage, or Wood Roasted Vegetables, or Hickory Smoked Ham (omit gravy), or Lobster without butter.

4700 Camp Bowie Blvd.
Fort Worth, TX 76107
817/738-4761

LUCILE'S MEAT LOAF *with Tomato Sauce*

This is a traditional Willis family recipe, with the exception of the Italian tomato sauce. The substitution still makes Willis's mother cry.

1 1/2 pounds ground beef
   3 slices soft white bread, torn into very small pieces
1/2 cup ketchup
1/2 cup finely diced onion
   2 tablespoons chopped parsley
   1 egg, beaten
   1 teaspoon salt
1/4 teaspoon black pepper
   2 cups tomato sauce (recipe follows)

ITALIAN TOMATO SAUCE
   2 tablespoons olive oil
1/2 cup minced yellow onion
   2 tablespoons minced garlic
1/4 cup tomato paste
1/4 cup red wine
   2 pounds plum tomatoes, chopped
   3 sprigs fresh basil, stemmed and chopped
   3 sprigs fresh thyme, stemmed and chopped
1/2 cup chicken stock
   1 bay leaf
     Salt and white pepper to taste

Mix all ingredients except tomato sauce, thoroughly. Press into 9x5x3-inch loaf pan. Bake uncovered at 350 degrees for about 1 1/2 hours. Remove from oven and drain off excess fat. Cut into slices 1 inch thick. Pour 1/3 cup sauce on warmed service plates. Place meat loaf on sauce and drizzle more sauce over the top. Serve with mashed potatoes and peas and carrots. *Serves 5.*

Italian Tomato Sauce
Heat oil in pan, sauté onions briefly over low heat. Add garlic and sauté. Add tomato paste and cook mixture slowly into a thick paste, about 2 to 3 minutes. Deglaze pan with wine and add all remaining ingredients. Simmer for 45 minutes. Cool briefly, then puree in blender or food processor and strain. Leftover tomato sauce may be served with pasta, fish, poultry or any meat, or frozen for future use. *Yields 5 cups.*

 Choose extra-lean ground beef or use 1/2 veal and 1/2 beef. Place on a rack in the pan to cook away fat. Use 2 egg whites for the whole egg. To increase fiber, substitute 2/3 cup oatmeal or oat bran, or whole wheat bread.

 Simi Altaire (California Red)
Glass Mountain Cabernet Sauvignon (California Red)

CRAB CAKES *with Roasted Garlic Sauce*

The key to exceptional crab cakes is fresh lump crabmeat. These freeze well. Make a double recipe and keep some on hand for impromptu entertaining.

  5 pounds fresh lump crabmeat
  4 cups soft white bread crumbs
  5 large eggs, lightly beaten
  1 1/4 cups mayonnaise
1/3 cup prepared mustard
  2 tablespoons Worcestershire sauce
1/4 cup minced parsley
  1 tablespoon white pepper
      Dash Tabasco
1/4 cup oil or butter

ROASTED GARLIC SAUCE
  6 heads garlic
  2 tablespoons olive oil
  4 cups mayonnaise
  3 tablespoons lemon juice
  1 teaspoon white pepper
  1 teaspoon garlic powder
      Salt to taste

Carefully pick over crabmeat and remove all shell and cartilage. Leave crab in large lumps. Gently mix in bread crumbs. Combine egg, mayonnaise, mustard, Worcestershire, parsley, pepper and Tabasco. Gently blend with crabmeat mixture. Form crab mixture into 4-ounce patties. Add butter or oil to saute pan and heat until oil ripples but does not smoke.

Cook crab cakes, browning on both sides and turning only once. Uncooked crab cakes may be refrigerated until the next day, or frozen until needed. Place 2 crab cakes on serving plate and spoon a small amount of sauce over each. *Makes 30 crab cakes.*

Coat garlic heads in oil, then wrap in foil. Bake at 350 degrees for 45 minutes, or until garlic becomes soft. Remove peel from garlic, squeezing out as much of the pulp as possible, and combine with remaining ingredients in food processor. Sauce may be made 3 to 4 days in advance. Cover and refrigerate. *Yields 4 cups.*

 Substitute 10 large egg whites for the 5 eggs. Use reduced-fat mayonnaise for crab cakes and sauce, and prepare only half of the sauce. Use only 1 tablespoon oil to roast garlic. Bake the crab cakes instead of frying to omit 1/4 cup oil.

 Beringer Meritage (California White)
Llano Estacado Sauvignon Blanc (Texas White)

EMERALD COAST FISHERMAN'S STEW

Willis invented this dish out of necessity while cooking on Florida's Emerald Coast (the Panhandle). The balance of curry, cream and tomato is unique.

1/2 pound salmon,
    cut into 1/2-inch cubes
1 pound red snapper,
    cut into 1/2-inch cubes
1 pound shrimp,
    cut into 1/2-inch cubes
1 pound swordfish,
    cut into 1/2-inch cubes
2 cups 1/4-inch diced onions
1 cup 1/4-inch diced carrots
1 cup 1/4-inch diced celery
2 cups 1/4-inch diced potatoes
3 tablespoons olive oil
1 cup white wine
2 cups fresh or canned tomatoes,
    peeled, seeded and diced
1 cup cream
1 tablespoon curry powder
1 tablespoon black pepper
1 tablespoon salt
2 1/2 cups chicken stock
8 whole shrimp, steamed (for garnish)
    Chopped parsley (for garnish)

Steam seafood for 3 to 6 minutes, reserve and keep warm. In a large saucepan, saute onions, carrots, celery and potatoes in olive oil. Add all other ingredients except seafood. Simmer 20 minutes. Add seafood, heat through, and serve warm. *Serves 4.*

 Seafood is healthy, but can be high in fat. Cut amounts in half, and sauté with Pam and 1 tablespoon olive oil. Use evaporated skim milk instead of cream. Omit salt.

 St. Andrews Chardonnay (California White)
Markham Sauvignon Blanc (California White)

RANCH GOAT CHEESE CANAPÉS

TEXAS BOBWHITE QUAIL
with Jalapeño Kumquat Sauce

RANCH PRALINES

SUNSET RANCH™ MARGARITA

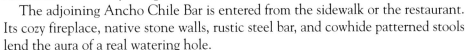

The ranch was never so stylish as at Michaels. Chef Michael Thomson's "contemporary ranch cuisine" is far from the original chuckwagon grub of Texas cowboys. The contemporary theme extends from the restaurant's kitchen to its art-gallery decor. With partner John Kennedy, Thomson has created a sleek and sophisticated environment where the Cowtown chic come to see and be seen.

Thomson's cuisine combines prime cuts of beef, chicken, and fish with spices indigenous to the Southwest. "Our customers' favorites are the Pan-Seared Tenderloin, Goat Cheese Tart, Tortellini Margherita, and Jalapeño Shrimp," says Thomson. "The Gulf Crab Cakes, a house specialty, are very popular, and our featured fish entrees are always a big hit."

The adjoining Ancho Chile Bar is entered from the sidewalk or the restaurant. Its cozy fireplace, native stone walls, rustic steel bar, and cowhide patterned stools lend the aura of a real watering hole.

Kennedy says, "Our wine list is exclusively American, with special Zinfandels selected to complement the spicy nature of the food. We offer twenty wines by the glass."

Michaels also serves a Germain-Robin brandy and an Iron Horse cuvee under the restaurant's private label. The Ancho Chile Bar offers the full menu and a special collection of Texas tapas.

When asked the secret of his success, self-taught Thomson replies, "My food philosophy is simple: All food should be of its essence. Its flavor should be maximized, and it should be presented as naturally as possible. I try to put an interesting twist on everything I do, with the essence of the item as the star, not supplemental ingredients or an overdone artistic presentation." His advice for home cooks: The size and heat of chiles can vary substantially. You can always add more chile heat, but you can't take it away.

Thomson is working hard to attain fame for the restaurant. "We want three stars in Texas Monthly, to earn a DiRoNA award, and to be one of "Food & Wine" Magazine's awarding-winning chefs."

LIGHTER BITES

Select from Texas Bobwhite Quail, Jalapeño Shrimp, the House or Tumbleweed Salad with dressing on the side, Michaels Garden Vegetable Plate, Oven Roasted Chicken, Citrus Salmon, or a 4 to 6 ounce portion of Ancho Beef Steak.

3413 West Seventh Street
Fort Worth, TX 76107
817/877-3413

RANCH GOAT CHEESE CANAPÉS

Stirado Rolls from the Massimo da Milano Bakery in Dallas make the best croutons.

24 - 1/4-inch thick baguette slices
4 Roma tomatoes sliced 1/4-inch thick
1/2 cup fresh cilantro, minced
   Cracked pepper

ROASTED GARLIC PUREE
1 cup fresh garlic cloves, peeled
1 1/2 teaspoons olive oil

CILANTRO PESTO
3 garlic cloves
1/4 cup grated Parmesan cheese
3 cups chopped fresh cilantro
1/2 cup pecan pieces
1/4 cup olive oil
1 teaspoon black pepper

RANCH GOAT CHEESE MIX
1/2 pound cream cheese
1/2 pound fresh goat cheese
1/4 cup roasted garlic puree
1 tablespoon dry Hidden Valley Ranch Dressing Mix

RASPBERRY VINAIGRETTE
1 cup raspberries, fresh or frozen
4 tablespoons sugar
2 tablespoons water
2 tablespoons Dijon mustard
1/4 cup red wine vinegar
1 tablespoon each salt, pepper, Italian herb blend, Maggi seasoning
1 cup olive oil

For garlic puree, coat garlic with oil and season with salt. Wrap in foil and bake at 375 degrees for 45 minutes. Puree. Combine all pesto ingredients, except oil, and puree. Drizzle in oil with processor running.

Combine goat cheese mix ingredients in food processor until well blended. Cheese mixture may be refrigerated for several days. Bring to room temperature to assemble.

Place raspberries, sugar and water in a saucepan and simmer into a syrup. Cool briefly and place in blender with all vinaigrette ingredients except oil. With blender running drizzle in oil until dressing is emulsified. Strain.

To assemble the canapés, spread a thin layer of pesto on each crouton. Place in 350-degree oven for 3 to 4 minutes to lightly toast the croutons. Remove and cool.

Place a slice of tomato on the pesto. With a pastry bag, pipe a small amount of cheese onto the tomato. Top with fresh cilantro and cracked pepper. Drizzle with a small amount of vinaigrette and serve within the hour. Makes 24 pieces.

 Cap Rock Brut (Texas Sparkling Wine)
McDowell Grenache Rosé (California Rosé)
Sterling Sauvignon Blanc (California White)

TEXAS BOBWHITE QUAIL *with Jalapeño Kumquat Sauce*

Quail may be purchased at Michaels.

6 Texas bobwhite quail
1 teaspoon each salt and black pepper
6 fresh jalapeño chiles
18 kumquats, halved, or 2 oranges, sliced

QUAIL MARINADE
1/2 cup red wine
2 tablespoons red wine vinegar
1/4 cup prepared teriyaki sauce
1 teaspoon ancho chile powder
1/2 teaspoon powdered ginger
1 teaspoon freshly ground black pepper
1 teaspoon granulated garlic
1 cup corn oil

JALAPEÑO KUMQUAT SAUCE
1 tablespoon corn oil
2 tablespoons chopped shallots and garlic
6 fresh kumquats or 1 small orange, chopped
1 tablespoon chopped fresh jalapeño chiles
1/4 cup red wine vinegar
2 teaspoons jalapeño chile powder (Pendery's)
2 cups orange juice concentrate
1/3 cup natural honey
1 1/2 cups reduced veal stock
Salt and freshly ground black pepper

Combine marinade ingredients and mix well. Coat each quail thoroughly and marinate for 24 hours. Drain for several minutes before cooking.

Lightly salt and pepper each quail. Grill, turning once, until cooked medium. At the same time, grill the jalapeños and kumquats. Make attractive grill markings on the quail, chiles and kumquats.

Place one quail, one jalapeño, and 6 pieces of kumquat on each plate. Ladle 1/4 cup sauce over the quail. Garnish with fresh herbs. *Serves 6.*

Jalapeño Kumquat Sauce
Heat oil in a small, heavy saucepan. Add shallots, garlic, kumquats, and jalapeños. Season with salt and pepper. Sauté until the garlic is golden. Add vinegar and simmer until almost dry. Add jalapeño chile powder, orange juice, honey and veal stock. Simmer until reduced to 2 1/2 cups. The sauce should lightly coat the back of a spoon. Strain through a very fine strainer. Correct seasoning. Keep warm until served. *Yields 2 1/2 cups.*

Beringer Merlot (California Red)
Sonoma-Cutrer Chardonnay (California White)
Estancia Sangiovese (California Red)

RANCH PRALINES

These tasty morsels can be crumbled onto any dessert for instant impact.

2 cups granulated sugar
1 cup brown sugar
2 tablespoons corn syrup
6 tablespoons butter
1 cup milk
2 dashes salt
2 tablespoons ancho chile powder
1 cup pecans
1/2 cup Kahlúa

Mix first seven ingredients in a saucepan. Over low heat, cook until mixture almost boils. Stir for 2 minutes more at nearly boiling. Cover and cook for 3 minutes. Then uncover and cook until temperature reaches 250 degrees on a candy thermometer.

Let cool to 200 degrees. Stir in pecans and Kahlúa. Drop by tablespoons onto wax paper. *Makes 4 dozen pralines.*

SUNSET RANCH™ MARGARITA

Ask Michaels bartender for their special cactus pear puree to take home. The mix is available in local markets.

1 cup Patron añejo tequila
1/2 cup Citronge liqueur
2 cups Ranch Margarita Mix
(recipe follows)

RANCH MARGARITA MIX
1/3 cup water
1/3 cup sugar
1 cup cactus pear puree
1/3 cup fresh lemon juice
1/3 cup fresh lime juice

Dissolve sugar in water over heat to make simple syrup. Combine cactus pear puree, juice and simple syrup and mix well to prepare margarita mix. Shake Ranch Margarita Mix with tequila and liqueur, then pour over ice. For an Original Ranch Margarita, use Coyote tequila, orange liqueur and Ranch Margarita mix. Garnish with lime wedge and enjoy. *Makes 6 margaritas.*

CHICKEN HUNTER STYLE
DUKE OF WINDSOR SANDWICH
NM PASTA GIOVANNI
POPOVERS
NEW MEXICO SANDWICH

From accessories to Zodiac, from formals to fortnight, from rodeo to Rodéo, Neiman Marcus has brought couture to Cowtown for thirty years.

The store's ambiance was always enhanced by fine dining in its restaurant. NM Cafe offers the ever-popular popovers of the past with New Mexico Sandwiches of now, and the daily Discovery luncheon. The hungry shopper, the mall-hopper, and the ladies who lunch are all present. Some new features and faces can be counted on to make dining a most pleasurable experience.

One new feature is an expanded menu. The classic "Medley" of tea sandwiches and soup is still here, paired with more choices and new approaches.

Manager Wes Glover notes, "The white tablecloths have been removed, and aprons and Oxford shirts on the waiters reflect a more relaxed atmosphere. Our prices are very reasonable. We have been able to bridge the gap."

And speaking of bridge, models offer show-and-tell styles from the bridge and other departments throughout the store. That isn't the only style show, though. NM Cafe draws people from all walks and talks of life with its new attitude. From TCU Greek-speak to Stock Show livestock lingo, from Calvin Klein and Crisca to boots and belt buckles, NM Cafe sports it all.

The NM Cafe decor is as flexible as the crowd it serves. Its Wedgewood blue walls wear innovative art, and the sound system serves smooth jazz. Flowers in the enclosed courtyard and tiny tree lights brighten the view on cloudy days. Wood and brass dividers break the restaurant into separate dining areas.

Glover has marshaled kitchens and restaurants at Neiman Marcus for thirteen years. He inherited his love and talent for food from his mother. "She is a fabulous cook," he says. It certainly shows in NM Cafe.

Neiman Marcus has compiled a cookbook of the Cafe's favorite meals. "Pure & Simple," full of Neiman Marcus tradition, brings time-honored favorites to home cooks.

LIGHTER BITES

Enjoy a fruit salad with cottage cheese, or Baked Salmon, Chicken Caesar, or Warm Chicken Salad with sauces on the side, a Duke of Windsor without cheese, or the NM Chicken Olé without guacamole.

Neiman Marcus
2100 Green Oaks Road
Fort Worth, TX
817/738-3581

NEW MEXICO SANDWICH

This southwestern-style sandwich with its hot bite and soothing chutney mayonnaise evokes images of its namesake.

> 1 tablespoon mayonnaise
> 1 tablespoon Major Grey chutney
> 2 slices French bread, toasted
> 1-2 pieces leaf lettuce
> 2 thin slices tomato
> 2 slices bacon, cooked until crisp
> 2-3 ounces sliced, smoked turkey breast
> 2 slices pepper jack cheese

Mix mayonnaise and chutney, and spread on both slices of toast. Layer lettuce, then tomatoes, bacon, smoked turkey, and pepper jack cheese on one slice of toast. Top with remaining toast and cut sandwich into 3 long fingers. Serve with Texas caviar (black-eyed pea relish) and tomatillo relish. *Serves 1.*

 Serve mayonnaise on the side, or substitute mustard. Omit bacon. Use only 1 slice of Monterey Jack cheese, or omit the cheese altogether.

 Simi Chardonnay (California White)
Ravenswood Zinfandel (California Red)

FACING PAGE
Whistle Stop
Giuliano Casulli, left, Cherif Brahmi, Mike Leatherwood.

FOLLOWING PAGE
Top of the World
Sterling Steves, left, Bernard Tronche, Jean Louis Barrére.

OLD SWISS HOUSE COLD CUCUMBER SOUP
VEAL OSCAR A LA ROSSEL
LES CREVETTES D'ESPAGNE SOUFFLE A LA FINANCE
FILET WELLINGTON A LA SENNHAUSER

Thirty years ago Fort Worth embraced the classic cuisine of the Old Swiss House. Today, Chef Walter Kaufmann's cheerful greeting comforts newcomers and envelops regular customers.

Experienced, tuxedo-clad waiters and a European wine list enhance the light and trendy lunch. A more classic dinner menu offers sumptuous veal, steaks and seafood that precede fabulous desserts. High ceilings and impeccable service abound in this modern atmosphere of elegance, which also serves a beautiful view of the Trinity River.

Old Swiss House

Kaufmann honors three colleagues for their talent and accomplishments by including a recipe from each. Willy Rossel, Josef Sennhauser and Charles Finance each contributed a recipe. The men have quite a history together — their friendship has spanned six decades and two continents.

As a teenager in Lucerne in the 1940s, Kaufmann studied under Finance. Sennhauser, then the head chef of the Baur au Lac Hotel in Zurich, met Finance while participating in yearly sporting events in the mid-40s. By 1950, Finance had moved to the United States. As Executive Chef of Western Hotels, he led the first American team to the Culinary Olympics in Bern. There he met Rossel, leader of the Zurich team.

Rossel moved to the Hotel Caribe in Puerto Rico in 1952. Finance replaced him. Upon coming to Fort Worth's Ridglea Country Club in 1955, Finance was delighted to find Kaufmann here. Sennhauser was lured to Ridglea from the Baur au Lac in 1956. And in 1958 Rossel moved to Dallas to open the Sheraton. That year Finance authored his only book written in English, "Buffet Catering."

The 1960s found all four Swiss chefs in Texas. Kaufmann opened the Old Swiss House in 1964, while Sennhauser was Executive Chef at Ridglea Country Club. Rossel joined Braniff Airlines in 1965 as director of food service planning.

The four friends gather often to share good food, good wine, and good memories. These days Rossel still does consulting work; Finance raises orchids; Sennhauser plays golf; and Kaufmann continues to create fabulous cuisine at one of Fort Worth's most beloved restaurants, the Old Swiss House.

LIGHTER BITES

Select from Shrimp Cocktail, Orange Roughy without butter, Fresh Salmon, the Lady's Tenderloin or Broiled Lamb Chops With Mint Jelly, or Pork Chop with Cherry Sauce on the side.

1541 Merrimac Circle
Fort Worth, TX 76107
817/877-1531

OLD SWISS HOUSE COLD CUCUMBER SOUP

Kaufmann's quick soup satisfies any time of the year.

   4 large cucumbers
   4 tablespoons butter
   2 large yellow onions, sliced
   4 cups chicken stock
1/2 cup flour
   1 cup each milk and cream
   1 teaspoon lemon juice
1/16 teaspoon cayenne pepper
1/4 teaspoon salt (optional)

Peel, seed and chunk the cucumbers. Sauté onions until transparent and add cucumbers and chicken stock. Boil, and then simmer until cucumbers are soft. Blend flour and milk together until smooth. Whisk into soup and let boil for 10 minutes. Press soup and cucumbers through a sieve or food mill. Add remaining ingredients. Refrigerate. Garnish with fresh chives. *Serves 6.*

 Substitute 1 tablespoon margarine, and use skim milk and evaporated skim milk to sharply reduce calories and fat.

 Chalk Hill Sauvignon Blanc (California White)

VEAL OSCAR A LA ROSSEL

Willy Rossel has circled the globe as a chef, influencing the cuisine of the world's great hotels.

   1 pound veal tenderloin
    Salt and pepper
3/4 cup flour (divided use)
   8 tablespoons butter (divided use)
   8 small Danish lobster tails (scampi)
   2 teaspoons lemon juice (divided use)
   1 egg, beaten
3/4 cup cream, heated
2/3 cup sliced mushrooms
   1 tablespoon dry sherry
1/2 cup prepared béarnaise sauce
 16 asparagus spears, steamed
   2 tomatoes, halved and grilled

Season veal with salt, pepper, and paprika, and dredge in 1/2 cup flour. Sauté. Devein scampi. Season with salt, pepper, and 1 teaspoon lemon juice. Dip in egg, flour and saute. Melt remaining butter and flour. Add cream, mushrooms, salt, pepper, lemon juice and sherry.

Put mushrooms on plates and top with veal and scampi and béarnaise. Garnish with asparagus and tomatoes. *Serves 4.*

 Sauté veal with just 1 tablespoon margarine. Substitute egg whites for yolks and evaporated skim milk for cream, and use 1/4 cup béarnaise sauce.

 Sanford Pinot Noir (California Red)
Saintsbury Carneros Pinot Noir (California Red)

LES CREVETTES D'ESPAGNE SOUFFLÉ A LA FINANCE

Charles Finance, author and former worldwide executive chef for Greenbrier, Hilton Hotels and other hotel chains, taught this author the best of classic cuisine.

8 large raw red Spanish shrimp,
   scampi, or jumbo shrimp
1/8 teaspoon salt
1/16 teaspoon pepper
1 tablespoon lemon juice
1 teaspoon Worcestershire sauce
1/4 cup fish broth (from bouillon cubes)
1/4 cup dry white wine

CREAMY LEEK SAUCE
1 leek, white part only
2 teaspoons butter
1/2 teaspoon cornstarch, liquefied with
1 tablespoon sherry
1 cup fish stock or chicken broth
1/2 cup heavy cream
   Dash of salt and white pepper

LOBSTER MOUSSE
3 1/4 ounces raw lobster meat
1/2 cup plus 2 tablespoons heavy cream
1 egg white
1/4 teaspoon salt
   Dash Tabasco or pinch
   cayenne pepper
2 teaspoons cognac

FINAL GLAZING (GLACAGE)
1 cup prepared hollandaise sauce
2 teaspoons heavy cream, whipped
   Truffles, thinly sliced, for garnish

Clean shrimp, leaving on the tail fin. Butterfly and remove vein. Flatten the butterflied shrimp. Marinate for 1 hour in salt, pepper, lemon juice and Worcestershire sauce. Cut leek into a short julienne. Sauté slightly in butter. Mix in cornstarch mixture. Heat stock and cream, add leeks and stir until sauce thickens. Season with salt and white pepper. Set aside.

Cut lobster meat into pieces and place into food processor with 1/2 cup cream, egg white, salt, Tabasco and cognac. Puree. Add the remaining cream as the mousse thickens. The mousse must be light like a soufflé. Refrigerate until used.

Place mousse on the flattened shrimp, using a pastry bag fitted with a large, flat piping tip. Put fish stock and white wine in a buttered oven-proof dish. Add shrimp, cover with buttered parchment paper, and poach for 10 minutes in a 350-degree oven.

Prepare the glacage by mixing the hollandaise and whipped cream. To serve, put leek sauce on oven-proof plates, add shrimp and ladle glacage over the lobster mousse. Place plates under broiler for 1 minute to brown lightly. *Serves 4.*

 Substitute evaporated skim milk for all cream, margarine for butter, and use only half of the glacage.

 Raymond Chardonnay (California White)
Grgich Hills Fumé Blanc (California White)

FILET WELLINGTON A LA SENNHAUSER

Joseph Sennhauser, executive chef at Ridglea Country Club for 25 years, recommends purchasing puff pasty fresh from a bakery or frozen from a market.

1 5 to 6-pound beef tenderloin, trimmed and thin tip removed
1 teaspoon salt (divided use)
1 teaspoon pepper (divided use)
1/4 cup vegetable oil
1/4 cup butter
1 tablespoon finely chopped shallots
8 ounces mushroom caps, sliced
1/3 cup sherry
2 beef bouillon cubes, crushed
1 pound ground pork or veal
1 egg
1/8 cup paprika
   Pinch oregano
3-4 ounces canned goose liver pâté
2 medium truffles, chopped (optional)
20 ounces puff pastry
1 egg, beaten
2 cups demi-glace or brown sauce made from prepared mix
6 tablespoons sherry or Madeira wine
4 tablespoons butter

Sprinkle tenderloin with 1/2 teaspoon each of salt and pepper. Rub tenderloin with oil and roast in pre-heated 500-degree oven for 10 minutes. Set aside. To prepare topping, melt 1/4 cup butter, add shallots and sauté. Add mushrooms, sherry, and bouillon cubes, and cook until almost dry. Remove from heat and allow to cool slightly. Blend together the ground meat and egg. Add remaining salt and pepper, paprika, and oregano. Combine mushrooms and meat mixture. Mix thoroughly.

Remove filet from oven and make one 1/2-inch deep cut lengthwise down the meat. Fill the cut with pâté and truffle. Spread the mushroom mixture over the pâté and pack down firmly.

Quickly roll out the puff pastry and wrap the filet in dough, putting the seams on the bottom. Brush with beaten egg. Place on shallow pan and bake at 375 degrees for 25 to 30 minutes, or until internal temperature reaches 125 degrees and pastry is golden brown.

Heat demi-glace and sherry in a saucepan. Whisk in butter one tablespoon at a time. Keep warm. *Serves 10.*

Tip: Make stroganoff from the tip of the tenderloin.

 Omit oil from tenderloin, substitute 1 teaspoon margarine for butter, use only 1/2 pound ground veal, and 2 egg whites. Use only 1/2 teaspoon salt in recipe, wrap meat in phyllo dough, and omit butter from final sauce.

 Chateau Margaux (French Red)
Foppiano Petite Sirah (California Red)

LENTIL SOUP

LINGUINE
with White Clam Sauce

OSSO BUCCO

PROFITEROLES

Mediterranean breezes whisper through On Broadway and Portofino, where Italian meals and incredibly indulgent service prevail. "Independent restaurateurs make a priority of quality, service and value," says Reza Mirzadeh (meer-zah-day).

Like the cogs of a perfectly oiled wheel, the four Mirzadeh brothers brought special strengths into their partnership. Reza handles the business, Sam oversees details and creates recipes, and Hamid manages Portofino in Arlington. Their brother Josef left a legacy of energy and enthusiasm in the congenial atmosphere of the restaurants.

Portofino

The Mirzadehs agree that On Broadway is now far from its original concept. "We envisioned a simpler menu to serve movie-goers, but evolved to meet our customers' desire for a chic bistro," Reza says. On Broadway is most assuredly a bistro. The pink

ON BROADWAY Ristorente

walls, punctuated with neon lighting, bring unexpected energy to such an intimate restaurant. Its knowledgeable waiters in bright ties and long, white aprons whisk between cozy banquettes, bearing tantalizing plates of Italian food.

By contrast, Portofino's rich wood panelled walls glow with reflected candlelight. Deep, cozy chairs cluster around tables in the main dining room, and quiet conversation mutes the occasional clink of wine glasses. Its polished appearance and formal service belie the casual, comfortable nature of the restaurant.

House specialties include gourmet pizzas, Artichoke Romano, Linguini Puttanesca, and Cozze al Bredetto, and all pasta is homemade. Cap off the evening with cappucino or the Portofino Coffee, which is prepared tableside with a dramatic flambé technique. "Cappucino is a personalized drink, a conversation coffee to sip while enjoying your surroundings," Judie Mirzadeh says. Ornate, highly polished urns pour forth exotic espresso and frothy cappucino at each restaurant.

The family's devotion and enthusiasm for their restaurants is boundless. Hamid Mirzadeh says the family slogan could easily be "If my brothers say I can do it, it can be done."

ON BROADWAY
6306 Hulen Bend Blvd.
Fort Worth, TX 76132
817/346-8841

PORTOFINO
226 Lincoln Square
Arlington, TX 76011
817/861-8300

LIGHTER BITES

Select Seafood Salad or Peperoni Arrostiti, Artichoke Romano, mussels in marinara sauce, Capellini Pomodoro, Scampi Diavolo, lobster with linguine, or Vitello Pizzaiola.

LENTIL SOUP

This simple, nutritious soup is hearty enough to serve as a meal.

    2 cups lentils
    1 cup chopped onion
    1 cup chopped leek
    1 clove garlic, minced
    3 tablespoons olive oil
    1 teaspoon thyme
    2 bay leaves
    1 cup chopped celery
  1/2 cup diced carrots
    7 cups water
    2 teaspoons salt
       White pepper to taste

Rinse lentils and soak in boiling water to cover. In a large saucepan, sauté onion, leeks and garlic in oil until golden. Add thyme, bay leaves, celery and carrot and lower heat. Cover and cook for 5 minutes. Add water, salt, pepper and drained lentils and bring to a boil. Lower heat, cover, and simmer for about 1 hour. To serve, puree all, part, or none of the soup. Ladle into hot soup plates and garnish with chopped tomatoes. *Serves 8.*

 Antinori Chianti Classico Riserva (Italian Red)
Leeton Shiraz Merlot (Australian Red)

LINGUINE *with White Clam Sauce*

The smallest of the hard-shell clams, littlenecks have a diameter of less than 2 inches.

   32 littleneck clams
    1 cup white wine
    1 cup clam juice
  3/4 cup olive oil
  1/4 teaspoon crushed red pepper
    1 teaspoon each oregano and basil
    1 teaspoon chopped garlic
       Salt and pepper
1 1/2 pounds linguine pasta, cooked

In a stainless steel pot, combine clams, wine and clam juice. Bring to a boil, cover, and cook for 3 minutes or until the shells have opened. Drain, reserving liquid. Discard any unopened clams and reserve 12 for garnish. Shuck and chop remaining clams. Strain the liquid. In a sauté pan, heat oil, red pepper, oregano, basil and garlic. Add chopped clams and cooking liquid. Reduce by half and season. Serve over linguine. *Serves 4.*

 Sauté with 1 teaspoon oil plus Pam.

 Bolla Soave Classico (Italian White)
Gloria Ferrer Chardonnay (California White)

Osso Bucco

Order 1 1/2-inch thick veal shanks in advance from a reliable butcher.

- 4 10 to 12-ounce veal shanks, cut 1 1/2-inches thick
- 1 1/2 teaspoons salt (divided use)
- 1/2 teaspoon pepper (divided use)
- 1/2 cup flour
- 4 to 6 tablespoons olive oil
- 1 medium onion, chopped
- 2 medium carrots, chopped
- 1 cup chopped celery
- 2 garlic cloves, minced
- 2 cups dry white wine
- 1 cup veal or chicken stock
- 1 16-ounce can Italian peeled tomatoes, drained and chopped
- 2 tablespoons chopped parsley

Trim excess fat from veal. Season with 1 teaspoon salt and 1/4 teaspoon pepper. Dredge in flour and shake off excess. In a sauté pan, heat 2 tablespoons of the oil over medium heat and sauté veal until browned on all sides. Remove veal from pan and place in baking pan.

In same sauté pan, heat 2 tablespoons oil over medium heat. Add onion, carrots, celery, garlic and cook until soft. Add wine, broth, tomatoes, parsley and remaining salt and pepper. Bring to a boil and pour over veal shanks. Cover and bake at 350 degrees for 1 1/2 hours. *Serves 4.*

 Use only 1 tablespoon oil to sauté veal and 1 tablespoon to sauté vegetables.

 Lungarotti Rubesco (Italian Red)
Vietti Barolo (Italian Red)

PROFITEROLES

These cream-filled puffs can be made into a croquembouche, traditional at Italian wedding celebrations. Stack the puffs, which have been dipped in caramelized sugar syrup, in a pyramid.

   1 cup water
 1/4 cup butter
   1 cup all-purpose flour
   4 jumbo eggs
   1 cup heavy cream
   2 tablespoons powdered sugar
 1/2 cup chocolate syrup

Heat oven to 400 degrees. Grease and flour cookie sheet. Place water and butter in a 2 1/2 quart saucepan and bring to a boil. Stir in flour. Stir vigorously over low heat about 1 minute, or until mixture forms a ball. Remove from heat and cool 5 minutes. Beat in eggs, one at a time, beating each time until smooth.

Drop 2 inches apart by tablespoons onto the cookie sheet, to make about 18 puffs. Bake approximately 25 minutes or until puffed and golden brown. Cool. Gently slice off tops and reserve. Pull out any pieces of soft dough.

Beat heavy cream and powdered sugar in a chilled bowl until stiff. Fill puffs with whipped cream and replace tops. Mound puffs on a large serving plate. Refrigerate 1 hour or until the dessert is firm. Top with chocolate syrup and serve. *Serves 6.*

 Use Pam to grease pan, substitute margarine and egg substitute, omit cream and sugar and use light non-dairy topping and prepared fat-free chocolate syrup.

 Capezzana Vin Santo (Italian Dessert Wine)
Fontanafredda Asti Spumante (Italian Sparkling Wine)

ANGEL HAIR PASTA WITH SEA SCALLOPS
MUSSELS ALLA MARINARA
ALASKAN SALMON IN BASIL AND CREAM
ROASTED PEPPERS
BROILED VEAL CHOPS
CREAM CARAMEL

For those who have never seen the Italian Riviera, a visit to Arlington's Piccolo Mondo may be the next best thing. With its warm-toned interior, slowly oscillating ceiling fans and fresh, authentic cuisine, it's no stretch of the imagination to picture a white beach and sparkling sea beyond the shuttered windows.

Piccolo Mondo touts a traditional Italian style with its relaxed ambiance and reasonably-priced cuisine. Patrons of this romantic sampling of Italy are greeted with a wide smile by co-owner Antonio Capaccioli. He and his partner, Executive Chef Nick Saracino, both native Italians, opened Piccolo Mondo in 1983. It is

PICCOLO MONDO

one of Tarrant County's most romantic trattorias with a cozy candlelit atmosphere, live piano music, and a whimsical menu.

The restaurant draws a bustling business crowd for lunch. They come for Sausage and Peppers with Marinara Sauce, and Breaded Chicken Breast with Eggplant Parmigiana and Mozzarella. Request Antipasto or Tomato with Mozzarella for lighter lunch fare.

"Today, Italian food in restaurants is a mix of northern and southern Italian ingredients and dishes," Saracino says. "Only the home cook keeps regional traditions." He and his talented chefs, Giuliano Casulli and Antonio Baldera, are very particular about fresh ingredients. Every dish, including its sauce, is prepared for each individual order. Many of the delicate pastas are made in-house, and Saracino cuts his own meat to ensure perfection. The resulting components of each dish burst with individuality. The chef himself often selects the day's produce from the Dallas greengrocer. "It costs more time than money to get quality," he says.

Saracino's selectiveness is frequently the means for improving a dish. For instance, the secret to his best-selling gnocchi is simply in buying the right potato. "Many people use the wrong potato to make gnocchi," he says. "I tried it many times. You add more water, it gets too gluey; you add more flour, it gets too stiff. The difference is in the potato."

So, what is this secret potato? Saracino won't tell, but the delectable gnocchi are only a nod away at Piccolo Mondo.

LIGHTER BITES

Choose Mussels Marinara, Escargot alla Romana, or Minestrone soup, with Linguine & Red Clam Sauce, Scaloppine Marsala, or Scaloppine al Limone, Shrimp Provençal, Filet of Sole or Chicken alla Foresteira, with dressings and sauces on the side.

829 East Lamar Blvd.
Arlington, TX 76011
817/265-9174

BROILED VEAL CHOPS

Use thick loin or veal rib chops, and turn the meat only once.

    4 veal chops
      Salt and pepper
    1 pound mushrooms, finely chopped
    5 tablespoons butter, divided use
    2 garlic cloves, minced
    1 tablespoon chopped fresh parsley

Preheat broiler to 400 degrees. Flatten and score edges of veal chops, and season. Broil chops until light brown or to medium rare. Sauté mushrooms in 4 tablespoons butter and garlic. Garnish chops with mushrooms and parsley. *Serves 4.*

 Sauté mushrooms and garlic in 1/4 cup chicken broth. Omit butter and use Pam.

 Tinto Pesquera (Spanish Red)
Mastroberardino Taursai (Italian Red)

CREAM CARAMEL

Incredibly succulent, deliciously rich and oh, so satisfying.

  3/4 cup sugar, divided use
  1/3 cup water
    4 eggs, beaten
    1 teaspoon vanilla extract
    2 cups milk, heated to just under boiling

Combine 1/4 cup sugar with 1/3 cup water in a skillet. Cook over low heat, until syrup reaches a light brown color. Pour into 4 custard cups and set aside. Combine eggs and remaining 1/2 cup sugar in a bowl. Add vanilla and mix well. Gradually add milk, stirring rapidly until blended. Pour mixture over caramelized sugar into custard cups, filling almost to the top.

Place cups in baking pan. Add hot water to pan halfway up sides of cups. Bake at 375 degrees for 45 minutes. Cool and refrigerate.

 Substitute 1 cup Egg Beaters, and 1 cup skim milk plus 1 cup evaporated skim milk for zero fat.

 Piper Sonoma Brut (California Sparkling Wine)
Martini & Rossi Brut (Italian Sparkling Wine)

CHICKEN TCHOUPITOULAS
with Crawfish Hollandaise

GRILLED 'GATOR TAIL
with BBQ "Ouch" Sauce

JAMBALAYA

ROASTED REDSKIN POTATOES

Whatdeheck do Razzoo mean? The menu explains that a Razzoo is someone who thinks a styrofoam cooler is luggage. Those who frequent Razzoo's Cajun Cafe in Sundance Square know that it means authentic swamp-style fixings and a rip-roarin' good time.

You can expect the best Cajun food in town at Razzoo's. Louisiana Chef Scott Marks came here from New Orleans' top restaurants. Owner Mike Leatherwood boasts that the restaurant features anything that grows in a swamp.

"Scott is our resident Cajun," he says. "We develop the recipes together. He tells me what Cajun people eat, and I tell him what will sell here." With Fried 'Gator Tail, Rat Toes and Froggy Legs on the menu, who's to second guess?

Fire eaters will scream in delight at Razzoo's famous Hickory Grilled 'Gator Tail over Jambalaya Rice with BBQ "Ouch" Sauce. A plate of Rat Toes (fried jalapeños stuffed with crab and shrimp) may bring tears of emotion, and real hotheads should brave the Chicken Wings from Hell. Razzoo also translates to, "Don't get caught with an empty water glass."

The Cajun cravings of more sensitive palates need not fear. There are smoothly seasoned options, like Chicken Fais Deaux-Deaux, a Seafood Salad, and Mean Willie Green's Hickory Grilled Fish with Roasted Redskins. The Cajun favorite, Chicken Tchoupitoulas (chop-pa-too-las), is a hickory grilled chicken breast over smoked ham, potatoes and mushrooms, crowned with Crawfish Hollandaise Sauce.

From its Bayou decor of license plates, fishing poles with dangling lures, and lavish swags of Mardi Gras beads, to the animated menu, one never knows quite what to expect at this Cajun cafe. The late-evening atmosphere is spiced up by rollicking jazz and blues bands that set toes tapping at every table.

If you just can't get enough of Razzoo's charm in one sitting, it's okay — these folks will cater 'gator at your place. Marks jokes that it's wise to have a good smoke alarm.

LIGHTER BITES

Choose raw oysters, boiled crawfish or shrimp, Shrimp and Fish Creole, grilled fish or Barbecued Shrimp. Request blackened dishes with sauces on side or without butter.

318 Main Street
Fort Worth, TX 76102
817/429-7009

CHICKEN TCHOUPITOULAS *with Crawfish Hollandaise*

This famous swamp dish may be hard to say
(chop-pa-too-las), but it's a cinch to eat.

  1 cup salad oil
  1 teaspoon salt
  4 teaspoons paprika, and for garnish
  3 teaspoons cayenne pepper
  2 teaspoons each of white pepper,
     basil, onion and garlic powders
  4 7-ounce chicken breasts, butterflied
  4 tablespoons butter
  1 cup diced ham
  1 cup sliced fresh mushrooms
  1 cup chopped green onions
  1 tablespoon minced garlic
1 1/2 cups Crawfish Hollandaise

CRAWFISH HOLLANDAISE
  2 eggs, plus 1 egg yolk
1/4 teaspoon cayenne pepper
1/2 teaspoon each lemon juice,
     powdered chicken base and
     white wine
1/2 pound butter
1/4 pound margarine
2/3 cup chopped crawfish tail meat
  1 tablespoon minced fresh chives

Mix oil and spices, and marinate chicken for at least 1 hour. Salt and pepper chicken and place on oiled grill. Cook until done, turning once. Sauté ham, mushrooms, green onions and garlic in butter. Put on plates and top with chicken, hollandaise and paprika. *Serves 4.*

For hollandaise, combine eggs, egg yolk, cayenne, lemon juice, chicken base and wine in a blender. Melt butter and margarine in a saucepan and heat to 140 degrees (very hot). With blender running at medium speed, drizzle the butter mixture in slowly. Heat crawfish and chives in a non-stick skillet, then stir into sauce. *Yields 2 cups.*

 Substitute chicken broth or wine for oil in marinade, and use 1/2 tablespoon margarine for butter. Prepare sauce with egg substitutes, omit butter, or omit hollandaise altogether.

 Mezzocorona Pinot Grigio (Italian White)
Cypress Chardonnay (California White)

GRILLED 'GATOR TAIL *with BBQ 'Ouch' Sauce*

This hearty meal is a Cajun delight — unless you're an alligator. If you can't find 'gator meat, substitute rattlesnake or chicken.

- 1 pound alligator tail meat, thinly sliced
- 1 teaspoon cayenne pepper
- 2 cups BBQ "Ouch" Sauce (recipe follows)
- 8 cups fresh, hot Jambalaya (recipe follows)
- 4 tablespoons chopped green onions

BBQ 'OUCH' SAUCE
- 1/2 cup cornstarch
- 1 cup water
- 1/4 cup cayenne pepper
- 1/4 cup coarsely ground black pepper
- 2 tablespoons each of salt, crushed red pepper, thyme, and rosemary
- 1 1/2 teaspoons oregano
- 1/3 cup chopped garlic
- 1/3 cup Worcestershire sauce
- 6 cups seafood stock or fish bouillon
- 1 1/2 cups ketchup
- 1/4 cup Louisiana hot sauce
- 1 1/2 cups tomato sauce
- 3 pounds soft unsalted butter

Rub cayenne into meat, then marinate in 1/2 cup of BBQ "Ouch" Sauce for 1 hour. Cook over wood-burning grill until done. Place jambalaya in center of plate. Place alligator tail meat on top, and ladle BBQ "Ouch" Sauce on both sides of rice. Top with green onions. *Serves 4.*

Warm cornstarch and water over low heat for 5 minutes. Add remaining ingredients, except soft butter. Stir well. Slowly whip in softened butter until smooth. Cool in an ice water bath, stirring occasionally to keep the mixture from separating. *Yields 1 gallon.*

 Substitute 4 ounces margarine plus 5 1/2 cups chicken broth for butter, and omit salt.

 Marques de Murrieta Blanco Reserva (Spanish White)
Chappellet Chenin Blanc (California White)

JAMBALAYA

This Cajun dish is a treat alone or on the side.

    4 **tablespoons butter**
1/8 **cup diced, uncooked bacon**
    6 **ounces diced, cooked**
        Andouille sausage
1 1/2 **cups diced yellow onion**
    1 **cup each diced bell pepper, celery**
2/3 **cup diced cooked chicken**
1/2 **teaspoon each salt, cayenne pepper,**
        oregano, white pepper, thyme,
        minced garlic and crushed bay leaf
2/3 **cup diced tomatoes**
2/3 **cup tomato sauce**
    2 **cups seafood stock**
1/3 **cup chopped green onion**
1/4 **pound crawfish tails**
1/4 **pound popcorn shrimp**
2 1/4 **cups uncooked white rice**

Melt the butter. Add bacon and sausage and render or melt the fat. Sauté onion, bell pepper and celery. Stir in chicken and cook for 1 minute. Add seasonings and tomatoes and cook 5 minutes before adding tomato sauce, seafood stock and green onion. Heat to boiling and add crawfish tails, shrimp and rice. Reduce heat and simmer for 15 minutes, or until liquids are absorbed. *Serves 10.*

 Substitute margarine, drain cooked bacon and sausage, then sauté with vegetables in clean pan.

 Antinori Borro della Sala (Italian White)
Lockwood Chardonnay (California White)

ROASTED REDSKIN POTATOES

These spuds are a sure-fire complement to any swamp dish.

    2 **pounds red skin potatoes**
    2 **tablespoons vegetable oil**
    2 **tablespoons margarine**
1/4 **cup chopped yellow onions**
1/4 **cup chopped chives**
    1 **teaspoon each of salt, white pepper,**
        cayenne pepper, paprika,
        garlic powder, thyme and
        Prudhomme's vegetable seasoning

Cut potatoes into quarters and boil for 7 minutes. Drain and cool. Sauté onions and chives in oil and margarine. Cook until the onions begin to brown. Remove from heat. Mix spices and set aside. Pour onion mixture over potatoes and stir. Sprinkle on spices, and turn until evenly coated. Place potatoes on a sheet pan and cook at 350 degrees for 15 minutes or until slightly crisp. *Serves 6-8.*

 Use just 1/2 tablespoon each of oil and margarine.

 DeLoach Zinfandel (California Red)
Los Vascos Cabernet Sauvignon (Chilean Red)

VINE RIPE TOMATOES
with Fresh Mozzarella
FROZEN GRAND MARNIER SOUFFLÉ
FILLET OF SALMON NAPA VALLEY
GRILLED VEAL RIB-EYE BUGATTI

Seems like Jean Louis Barrére never gets to cook the hometown food. Before the chef of the Worthington's Reflections brought his classical French cuisine overseas, he ran a Paris restaurant where they served (imagine this) Tex-Mex.

Barrére recalls that two of his friends wanted to start a pizzeria. "I wasn't real big on the idea," he says. "So, I suggested opening up a Tex-Mex restaurant. The French people loved it."

As chef of The Worthington Hotel's elegant Reflections, he now caters to Cowtown's connoisseurs of fine food and wine. Barrére is bringing European influences into his menu creations. His background has prepared him well for that style. The versatile Frenchman trained at the Association Francais des Professionnel

Artisan, and honed his skills as sous chef of the famed Meridien Hotel in Paris.

After only months at the prestigious Worthington, Barrére has revised Reflections' menu and features a different international cuisine each month, including French, Spanish, Thai and British. As for daily specials, Barrére says he makes spontaneous decisions based on each day's allowances. Whatever the flavor, Barrére's effortless execution is classic and attractive. "French cuisine at its best is light and simple," he says. "It should be a regular indulgence, not a guilty pleasure reserved for special occasions."

Such talent abounds at the Worthington, which is a driving force in the community and the food industry. Food and Beverage Director Tim Foley said the hotel has developed a reputation for its quality cuisine and service. "We're the third largest in terms of hiring externs from CIA (Culinary Institute of America)," he says. "The Worthington has established a name, and apprentices want to come here."

Worthington newcomer Executive Chef Scott Gilbert, who comes from Michigan's four-star Amway Hotel, says he is enthusiastic about the move south. "I can see that what it took me two years to develop here (in Michigan) is already years in the making at The Worthington," he says. "We certainly have the talent to create a wonderful team flavor."

──────────── LIGHTER BITES ────────────

Design your dinner from Oysters Geoffrey, Seafood Fantasy, Tournedos "Belle of the Southwest" (omit lobster cream), Australian Lamb Dijonnaise or Bouillabaisse á la Marseilles.

The Worthington Hotel
200 Main Street
Fort Worth, TX 76102
817/870-1000

VINE RIPE TOMATOES *with Fresh Mozzarella*

Reflections prepares this Italian appetizer au gratin.

> 4 **large ripe tomatoes**
> 16 **thin slices fresh mozzarella**
> 1/2 **cup extra-virgin olive oil**
> 6 **cloves elephant garlic, lightly roasted**
> 1 **bunch each basil, chervil, chives, and Italian parsley**
> 4 **opal basil flowers for garnish**

Slice each tomato into 4 equal slices. Alternate with 4 mozzarella slices on an oven-proof plate. Broil until the mozzarella is melted. Sprinkle with pesto. To make the pesto, mix oil, garlic and herbs in a blender to a thick sauce consistency. *Serves 4.*

 Use just 2 tablespoons oil and substitute reduced-fat mozzarella. Recipe is rich in Vitamins A and C, folic acid and calcium, but has a lot of cholesterol and fat.

 St. Supery Sauvignon Blanc (California White)
Guenoc Chardonnay (California White)

FROZEN GRAND MARNIER SOUFFLÉ

This refreshing soufflé is great for entertaining.

SOUFFLÉ
> 1/3 **cup water**
> 1 **cup plus 2 tablespoons sugar**
> 6 **eggs, separated**
> 2 **teaspoons water**
> 1/2 **cup Grand Marnier**

CHANTILLY CREAM
> 1 **cup cold heavy cream**
> 1/3 **cup confectioners' sugar**
> 1/8 **teaspoon vanilla extract**

Mix water and sugar in heavy saucepan and cook to soft-ball stage (220 degrees). Whip egg whites until fluffy. Add syrup slowly, while whipping. Place egg yolks with water in saucepan and whisk over low heat until thickened. Mix in Grand Marnier. Fold in meringue. Place in refrigerator to chill.

For chantilly cream, beat powdered sugar into cream. Add vanilla and whip. Fold into meringue.

Wrap a 2-inch high wax paper collar around the inside of 6 individual soufflé molds. Pour mixture into mold and smooth the top. Freeze 6 hours. Remove wax paper before serving, and sprinkle with cocoa. *Serves 6.*

 Quady Essensia (California Dessert Wine)
Scharffenberger Brut (California Sparkling Wine)

FILLET OF SALMON NAPA VALLEY

This twist on salmon en papillote uses cabbage instead of paper, so the whole dish is edible.

16 large leaves of Napa cabbage
 4 6-ounce boneless fillets of
     Norwegian salmon
 1 cup red onion soubise
     (recipe follows)
 2 cups Cabernet Sauvignon
 4 large shallots, minced
1/2 cup heavy cream
 1 pound lightly salted butter
     White pepper

RED ONION SOUBISE
 1 large red onion, diced
 2 tablespoons butter
 2 tablespoons port wine
 1 teaspoon fresh rosemary
 1 cup heavy cream
     Salt and white pepper

Dip Napa cabbage leaves in boiling water for 30 seconds and drain. Remove center white rib. Lay 4 leaves out with the outer edges up and down, to make a sheet. Place the fillet of salmon in the center with red onion soubise on top. Fold the leaves up to cover the salmon and soubise. Repeat with remaining leaves and salmon fillets.

Place in a glass pan with shallots and Cabernet Sauvignon. Cover with foil. Place in a 350-degree oven for 10 to 12 minutes. Set fish aside and keep warm.

Remove the liquid to a small saucepan and reduce by half. Add cream and reduce by half again. Cut butter into 1-inch pieces. Add one piece at a time while whipping. Make sure each piece is melted before adding the next. Place sauce on a plate with cabbage-wrapped salmon on top, with the leaf pulled back to show the red onion soubise. *Serves 4.*

Sauté diced red onion with butter until golden brown. Add port and rosemary. Cook until dry. Add heavy cream. Cook until thickened. Season with salt and white pepper. Yields 1 cup.

 Omit sauce, or sauté onion with wine and 1 teaspoon margarine, and substitute evaporated skim milk for cream. With modifications, this healthy recipe is high in fiber, vitamins A and C, and minerals.

 Signorello Sauvignon Blanc (California White)
Bernardus Chardonnay (California White)

GRILLED VEAL RIB-EYE BUGATTI

Reflections' striking presentation of this dish resembles the Bugatti automobile.

    4 7-ounce boneless lean veal
       rib-eye steaks
   16 slices bacon
  1/2 cup balsamic vinegar
  1/4 cup white wine
  1/4 cup dry vermouth
    4 teaspoons freshly cracked
       black pepper
  1/4 cup heavy cream
  1/2 cup lightly salted butter
    8 ounces fresh spinach
    1 teaspoon butter
    4 sprigs fresh tarragon

Grill the veal steaks to medium on a wood-burning grill. Roll each slice of bacon into a wheel and skewer with a toothpick. Cook bacon in a 350-degree oven until almost crisp. Drain on a paper towel and remove toothpicks.

In a small sauté pan, place the vinegar, white wine, vermouth and pepper. Reduce by half over medium heat. Add heavy cream and reduce by half again. Cut butter into 4 equal parts. Whip in butter one piece at a time, making sure each piece has melted before adding the next.

Wilt the spinach in a sauté pan with 1 teaspoon butter. Place warm spinach in the center of each plate. Top with 2 wheels of bacon and place rib-eye on top. Top the steak with the balsamic vinegar-butter sauce. Garnish with a sprig of fresh tarragon. *Serves 4.*

 Use 4 to 5-ounce steaks, omit bacon, substitute evaporated skim milk and margarine, and wilt spinach in water or Pam.

 Franco Fiorina Barbaresco (Italian Red)
Domaine Drouhin Pinot Noir (Oregon Red)

FILET DE BOEUF DU SAINT-EMILION
AUMONIERE AU CRABE
STEAK DE THON AU POIVRE
MOULES AU PINEAU DES CHARENTES

In the quiet Monticello neighborhood, an A-frame building set back from Seventh Street is well-known by locals as the rustic and intimate country French restaurant, Saint-Emilion. Strangers might pass it by, without realizing that authentic fare from south of France has arrived in the southwestern United States.

Owner Bernard Tronche, a native of Saint-Emilion, could be called an ambassador of traditional dining. He recalls his childhood, where every meal was celebrated with the family together. His grandmother loved the happy faces of everyone eating, and his grandfather told stories about World War II and being in the French Resistance. "I miss this great family communication," Tronche says.

SAINT-EMILION

"We are not into merely feeding people, we are into dining — that's what food is all about," says Tronche, who worked under Guy Calluaud in Dallas. "If the customer understands food and his own lifestyle, and uses balance and not excess, he can have satisfaction at the table."

Native dishes near Tronche's heart include the Snails with Mushrooms and White Wine Sauce in a Puffed Pastry Crust, and Sautéed Veal Sweetbreads with Marinated Red Onions and Aged Wine Vinaigrette. Saint-Emilion's original salad with greens, walnuts and lardons was given to Tronche by his paternal grandfather. Roast Duck, or Whole Dover Sole with Artichoke Hearts and Capers complete the perfect Saint-Emilion meal.

Now that you are deep into the culinary delights, remember dinner isn't over until you've had dessert. Try the warm, crisp Apple Tart, Coffee Ice Cream Sundaes, Cream Caramel or the Chocolate Flourless Cake. According to Tronche, wine is an enjoyable part of a meal. "Put it on the table and don't make a big deal about it," he says. Enjoy Saint-Emilion's wine selections on the unique clipboard list, with choices from Bordeaux to California.

If food and wine options become overwhelming, Tronche himself will assist you. It is part of his savoir-faire as a French restaurateur, and what you would expect from an ambassador of traditional dining.

LIGHTER BITES

Select mixed lettuce salad with walnuts and lardons and dressing on side, turkey scaloppine with morels, lamb wrapped in eggplant, Dover sole with artichoke hearts and capers with lemon butter on the side, or accept the menu's offer to accommodate special dietary needs.

3617 West Seventh Street
Fort Worth, TX 76107
817/737-2781

FILET DE BOEUF DU SAINT-EMILION

At home in Saint-Emilion, Tronche would grill the steak over vine clippings and serve it topped with thinly sliced shallots mixed with the marrow and a little butter. This recipe calls for half a bottle of good Saint-Emilion wine — the other half is for the chef.

  5-6 **sections of a large beef bone with marrow**
1 3/4 **cups Saint-Emilion wine**
1 1/2 **teaspoons sugar**
  1/2 **cup beef stock**
      Pinch of dry thyme
    8 **tablespoons cold butter (divided use)**
    1 **tablespoon sunflower oil**
      Salt and pepper
    4 **6 to 8 ounce beef tenderloin steaks (tournedos)**
    2 **shallots, minced**

Poach the bone sections in a pan of simmering water for 5 to 7 minutes. Extract the marrow delicately, leaving the slices intact. Set aside and keep warm. Pour wine into a saucepan, add sugar and reduce by half. Add stock and reduce by one third. Add thyme. Melt 2 tablespoons butter in a skillet over high heat and add oil. Salt and pepper steaks and cook medium-rare or according to preference. Place on warmed platter.

Add 2 tablespoons butter and shallots to skillet and quickly sauté. Add wine sauce, reduce heat, and whisk in 4 tablespoons of cold butter, cut into pieces. Do not let the sauce boil.

Pour sauce onto steaks through a fine strainer. Top with the slices of marrow and garnish with Italian parsley. *Serves 4.*

 Omit marrow and use just 1 tablespoon margarine for butter.

 Chateau Haut-Bages Averous (French Red)
Far Niente Cabernet Sauvignon (California Red)
Chateau Cantenac Brown (French Red)

AUMONIERE AU CRABE

A delicious surprise package — these red bell pepper crêpes are stuffed with crabmeat and Boursin cheese and tied like a beggar's purse.

CRÊPE BATTER
  1 **large red bell pepper, roasted, peeled and seeded**
  1 **cup milk (divided use)**
  1 **tablespoon butter, melted and cooled**
  2 **eggs**
1 1/4 **cups flour**
 1/8 **teaspoon salt**
1/16 **teaspoon pepper**

FILLING
 12 **long fresh chives, dipped in boiling water for 10 seconds**
1/2 **cup Boursin cheese**
  1 **heaping cup fresh cleaned crabmeat**
    Salt and pepper

BASIL COULIS
  6 **tablespoons heavy cream**
1/3 **cup white wine**
  1 **cup lightly packed basil leaves**
    Salt and pepper

For crêpes, place bell pepper, 1/2 cup milk and butter in blender and puree until smooth. Add eggs, flour, salt, pepper and remaining milk. Blend to form a thin fluid batter. Let the batter rest for at least two hours. If the batter separates, stir to a smooth consistency. Make crêpes in a 6-inch non-stick skillet over medium heat. Lightly wipe hot skillet with butter and add about 3 tablespoons batter. Quickly move the skillet in a circle so batter spreads into a disk. Flip the crêpe once. Crêpes can be left at room temperature several hours. Place crêpes between paper towels or wax paper.

For the filling, mix crabmeat and Boursin. Season to taste. Place two tablespoons of filling in center of crêpe. Gather the crêpe around the filling to form a sack, and tie with a blanched chive.

For the coulis, cook cream and wine at a low boil for about three minutes. Cool to room temperature. Puree with basil in blender.

Warm filled crêpes. Serve on a pool of warm basil coulis. *Makes 12 beggar's purses.*

 Substitute skim milk, 1 teaspoon margarine, and Egg Beaters. Reduced-fat cream cheese could replace Boursin.

 Gratien Brut (French Sparkling Wine)
Domaine Weinbach Gewurztraminer (French White)

STEAK DE THON AU POIVRE

Buy sushi quality tuna. The center cut loin is best.

  4 **tuna steaks, 1 1/2 to 2 inches thick**
     Freshly cracked black pepper
  4 **tablespoons butter (divided use)**
  1 **cup heavy cream**
1/2 **cup veal stock**
  1 **shallot, minced**
  3 **tablespoons cognac**
1/4 **teaspoon salt**

Coat one side of each tuna steak with cracked peppercorns. Melt 2 tablespoons butter over high heat and sear the tuna steaks, peppered side down, for 2 minutes. Reduce heat, turn steaks, and cook like any other steak. Add salt. Remove tuna from skillet, place steak peppered side up on warm plates.

Add remaining butter to skillet, raise heat, and add shallots. Add cognac and flame. Add stock and cream, stir, and let thicken for 1 minute. Taste for seasoning and pour over steaks. *Serves 4.*

 Substitute 1/3 cup dry white wine for cream, and sauté fish and shallots with 1/2 tablespoon margarine each.

 Duboeuf Moulin-a-Vent (French Red)
Faiveley Mercurey (French Red)

MOULES AU PINEAU DES CHARENTES

This recipe is inspired by the regional apéritif, Pineau Des Charentes, which is available at local wine stores.

  1 **large egg yolk**
  2 **cups heavy cream**
     Salt and pepper
  2 **tablespoons butter**
  4 **shallots, minced**
  4 **pounds fresh black mussels,**
     unopened and cleaned
1/2 **cup dry white wine**
1/2 **cup white Pineau Des Charentes**
  1 **bay leaf**

Mix egg yolk into cream with salt and pepper. Melt butter in a large, lidded pot and sauté shallots until soft. Add mussels, wine, Pineau Des Charentes and bay leaf. Cook, covered, until mussels begin to open. Shake the pot occasionally. Add cream mixture and simmer slowly while remaining mussels open. Stir frequently. Do not boil or the egg will curdle. Taste for seasoning. Discard mussels that do not open. Serve in soup plates and sprinkle with parsley. *Serves 4.*

 Omit cream and egg yolk, and use only 1 tablespoon margarine to sauté shallots.

 Sterling Sauvignon Blanc (California White)
Orlando Jacob's Creek Sauvignon Blanc (Australian White)

RENIE STEVES

As CEO of Cuisine Concepts, Fort Worth's foremost food and wine consulting firm, Renie Steves has the tools to accomplish any culinary task. From the 6,000-plus volume library of cookbooks and reference materials, to the incredible array of pans and gadgets, Steves has equipped her domain to meet the exacting demands of a professional teacher, writer, food stylist and consultant — all of which she is.

A Certified Culinary Professional of the International Association of Culinary Professionals, Steves has studied under the world's finest teachers and chefs. She is active in Les Dames D'Escoffier, American Institute of Wine & Food, and is listed in Who's Who International Du Vin, and Who's Who in the South and Southwest. Last year she wrote "Dallas Is Cooking!" She and her husband, Sterling, write wine and leisure columns and free-lance feature articles under a dual byline.

For the last 15 years, Steves has set a fast pace at Cuisine Concepts. Five days in New York City for her equals 13 restaurant meals. She often works through the night, and it is tough for the staff to maintain her energetic tempo. "A good sense of humor is required around here," Steves says. "Some days I think we should be writing sit-coms instead of cookbooks!"

What one word sums up your work?
Taste. I am always tasting things. Creating recipes for the cooking school involves lots of tasting and testing. Sterling and I evaluate several wines each day, and I do a lot of menu consulting, which means analyzing the chef's practice run.

What is your biggest vice?
Table setting design and tableware are an important element of my work. I am inspired by the artistry of many pieces that I come across while traveling, and some are irresistible additions to my collection.

Who would you invite to the ultimate dinner party?
Socrates for the philosophical side, Winston Churchill for his diplomacy, Lyndon and Ladybird Johnson for a political point of view, Clark Gable for the romanticist in me, and my parents because they are a fascinating couple. Sterling would keep the conversation stirred up!

What is your best asset?
My supportive family — Sterling, who encourages me in every project; our children, who are patient and understanding; and the grandchildren, who add freshness, encouragement and laughter to our lives.

Please share your three best cooking tips:
1) High-quality herbs and spices are critical. We grow our own, and use Pendery's for dried items.
2) The smoker is your best friend for unique flavor and low-fat food.
3) Remember the French Paradox, and include a little wine with your meals for good health.

GEORGIA G. KOSTAS

Georgia G. Kostas

The Cooper Aerobics Center and Cooper Clinic stand in a park-like North Dallas setting. Georgia Kostas, MPH, RD, LD, and Director of Nutrition, founded the prestigious clinic's nutrition program in 1979. She is a renowned nutritionist, specializing in preventative and cardiovascular medicine, has authored "The Balancing Act Nutrition & Weight Guide" and co-authored "What's Cooking At The Cooper Clinic."

Kostas bounces into her office, glowing with youth and good health. She dons a starched lab coat, and faces the daily barrage of the good-health business. Her busy mailbox is divided into 'now,' 'today' and 'tomorrow' categories, and one knows everything will be done on time. The calendar is filled with patients' appointments, speaking engagements, professional conferences and civic events. Her warmth, kindness and generosity envelop visitors and co-workers, and the work flies quickly.

Kostas' five-star education and professional achievements include a B.A. in Biology from Rice University, a Master of Public Health in Nutrition from Tulane University School of Public Health and Tropical Medicine, and Residency in dietetics from Ochsner Hospital in New Orleans. She received the American Dietetic Association's "Sports and Cardiovascular Nutritionists National Achievement Award" in 1990. She is the ADA's liaison to the President's Council on Physical Fitness and Sports.

What do you do with your free time?
I love music, especially live music. I bicycle, and I'm happiest when I'm winning a tennis match.

What is your ideal vacation?
Something active and outdoors! Water sports, hiking, and biking, and long walks on quiet beaches.

What would you eat on this vacation?
I love traveling in Greece, and my favorite meal is a traditional Greek salad and Spanikopita, with peach cobbler a la mode for dessert.

What are your vices?
I love Godiva chocolates, eat on-the-go too often, and read food labels instead of novels.

What three health-conscious guests from history would you invite to dinner?
Lucille Ball for her humor and attitude, and Don Quixote for his idealism and belief in mankind, and James Beard, who is a fabulous chef.

THE BALANCING ACT *by Georgia Kostas, MPH, RD, LD*

Our earliest ancestors had very healthful diets. The ancient hunter-gatherers ate only the freshest, leanest meats and in-season fruits and vegetables. The radical changes in our civilization and lifestyle now give 'hunter-gatherer' new meaning: We must hunt for low-fat, healthful foods and gather nutrition knowledge from reliable sources. Good food with consistent exercise brings good health. It is possible to indulge in rich, unusual, and tantalizing foods by balancing them with the vast array of health wise choices.

The principles of balance are simple. The modern hunter-gatherer still has "plant" and "animal" foods. Plant foods, such as fruit, vegetables, whole-wheat bread, cereals, grains, rice, pasta and beans, are fiber-rich complex carbohydrates. Animal foods, such as lean meat, poultry, seafood, legumes, and cheese, are proteins. Two simple rules can help you create a personal blueprint for a lifetime of good health by balancing low-fat, high-fiber foods with richer choices.

3/4 RULE

3/4ths of your meal should be plant foods, and 1/4th should be animal foods.

RULE OF 80/20

Eating healthfully 80 percent of the time will permit some small splurges 20 percent of the time.

PRINCIPLES OF BALANCE

- Eat at least ten servings of plant foods each day.

- Variety and conservation are the keys to animal foods. Vary lean meat, poultry, seafood, legumes and cheese, and restrict protein intake to four to six ounces per day.

- Reduce the fat in your diet. Substitute vegetable fats such as margarine, and olive or canola oil for animal fats such as butter and cream. Limit oil, margarine, butter, mayonnaise, gravy, salad dressing and sauces to two tablespoons per day.

- Allow up to 4,000 milligrams of sodium per day. Beware of salt, soup, sauces, pickles, olives, hot dogs, ham, sausage, cheeses, chips, fast foods, snack foods, canned goods and commercial bakery products.

THE BALANCING ACT NUTRITION & WEIGHT GUIDE

Servings		Fiber (grams)	Fat (grams)	Sat Fat (grams)	Chol (mg)
3	Fruit	6	0	0	0
3	Vegetable	6	0	0	0
3	Grains	6-20	0-3	0	0
3	Starches	0-6	0-3	0	0
1	Protein	0	5-18	1-6	100-150
16-24 oz	Skim milk	0	0	0	5-10
1-2 T	Added Fat	0	10-30	0	0

The optimum diet is 50-60 percent complex carbohydrates and 20-30 percent fat. When counting fat grams, this translates to 20-30 grams of fat per 1,000 calories. Therefore, women would typically consume 1,600 calories with 35-50 grams of fat daily, and men 2,200 calories with 50-70 grams of fat.

RESTAURANT DINING BY DESIGN

Restaurateurs recognize their health-conscious patrons' concerns. The Lighter Bites in this book recommend some lower-fat choices from each menu. Choose rich items less frequently and in smaller amounts, or balance one rich selection with two lighter ones.

- Order grilled, broiled, baked, boiled and steamed food.
- Request less oil in every item.
- Order broth-based or tomato-based soups.
- Raw vegetables and raw seafood are good choices.
- Share entrees to reduce portion size.
- Request dressings and sauces on the side.
- Choose fresh fruit for dessert.

Spicy cuisines are a delicious alternative to fattening sauces. Add ginger, picante sauce, lemon juice, reduced-fat dressing or Italian spice blends instead of sauces or salt to cut calories, fat and salt.

HEALTH AT HOME

Imaginative planning and careful shopping can yield fabulous, healthy home cooked feasts. Strive for color and variety at each meal, and emphasize fresh, wholesome, unprocessed foods. Always read food labels and try to select items with zero to three grams of fat per 100 calories. Choose specialty products labeled reduced-calorie, low-fat, non-fat and fat-free. Certain foods are great additions to your diet:

- Omega-3 fatty acids in fish help lower cholesterol and prevent blood clotting. Shrimp and shellfish are almost fat-free, and a small serving is low in cholesterol.

- Buy "select" grade pieces of filet, tenderloin, flank, top round, and sirloin. Always trim excess fat and skin, and cook without added fat.

- Olive oil is considered a healthy oil because its fat is monounsaturated, and helps lower total cholesterol levels.

- Ounce for ounce, raw red peppers have four times more vitamin C than peeled oranges.

- Romaine, Boston and Bibb lettuces have up to six times as much vitamin C and eight times as much beta carotene as iceberg lettuce.

- Broccoli has just 45 calories per cup. One serving provides about 90 percent of the daily requirement of vitamin A (in the form of beta carotene), 200 percent of vitamin C, 10 percent of calcium, and 25 percent of daily fiber needs. Broccoli may protect against certain forms of cancer.

- Choose cantaloupe from the melon department. One cup meets the recommended daily allowance of vitamin A, and provides a substantial amount of vitamin C. Honeydew melon is not nearly so nutritious.

SENSIBLE SUBSTITUTIONS

When preparing a recipe at home, many common substitutions can be made to reduce calories, fat, cholesterol and sodium. These small modifications can often make the difference between an unhealthy recipe and a sensible meal.

● Substitute margarine for butter.

● Substitute 2 egg whites or 1/4 cup egg substitute for a whole egg.

● Use part-skim or reduced-fat cheeses. In cheese sauces, use skim milk and non-fat or low-fat cheese.

● Substitute canned evaporated skim milk for cream in thicker sauces, or use cornstarch for thickening if needed.

● Cocoa powder is fat-free and low in calories. Substitute 3 tablespoons cocoa plus 1/2 tablespoon oil per ounce of baking chocolate. Add a little sugar if needed for sweetness.

● Cut sugar in recipes and experiment with natural sweeteners such as vanilla, cinnamon, almond and cherry extracts, raisins, banana, berries, or concentrated apple juice.

THOUGHTFUL TECHNIQUE

Add less fat to your diet through cooking techniques.

❖ Broil, bake, steam, boil, grill and stir-fry.

❖ Sauté in a non-stick pan with vegetable cooking spray, broth, vegetable or fruit juice, or wine.

❖ Use vegetable cooking spray to grease pans and glaze pastry.

❖ Reduce the amount of oil in a recipe. Replace oil in cakes with an equal amount of applesauce, non-fat yogurt or low-fat buttermilk.

Good health contributes immensely to one's overall enjoyment of life. Your personal balancing act can enrich each day, so choose wisely. I wish you a lifetime of good health and good food.

Georgia G. Kostas

NUTRITIONAL ANALYSIS*

	Portion of Recipe	Calories		Fat (grams)		Saturated Fat (grams)		Cholesterol (milligrams)		Sodium (milligrams)		Dietary Fiber (grams)	
		O	M	O	M	O	M	O	M	O	M	O	M
Bella Italia West													
Tuna Alla Grappa	1/2	610	375	27	13	5	3	104	63	240	200	0	0
Ostrich 3G	1/2	435	330	25	11	12	4	126	85	485	350	0	0
Linguine Carbonara	1/4	1060	600	71	8	36	1	190	25	345	755	3	3
Pappardelle Allo Struzzo	1/4	660	550	23	11	9	5	65	51	830	625	3	3
Prosciutto e Melone	1/2	150		6		3		30		705		1	
Mascarpone/Raspberry Sauce	1/4	455		40		25		128		340		3	
Bistro Bagatelle													
Bavarois of Salmon	1/6	680	400	67	34	33	7	150	19	670	735	1	1
Salade/Pommes de Terre	1/4	775	370	73	29	7	3	0	0	80	80	5	3
Chocolate Marquise	1/10	380		31		19		134		95		4	
Le Blanc/Poulet/Au Pistou	1/4	365	265	26	15	6	3	87	78	225	245	1	1
Cacharel													
Chilled Cantaloupe Soup	1/4	150		1		0		0		30		3	
Wild Rice Cake	1/6	40		1		0		0		65		1	
Roasted Loin of Lamb	1/4	245	230	13	11	4	4	74	74	390	390	1	1
Saffron Sorbet	1/6	100		0		0		0		1		0	
Broiled Sea Scallops	1/4	800	350	63	11	8	2	56	56	560	560	6	6
Cactus B & G													
Grilled Vegetable Tortilla Roll	1/6	280	225	16	8	2	1	0	0	495	635	4	4
Pork Loin/Relish/Sauce	1/6	480	415	25	17	7	6	136	136	260	260	2	2
Wild Turkey Roll	1/6	440	390	17	11	7	5	144	136	700	600	3	3
Adobe Club Sandwich	1/6	900	650	42	15	6	3	78	78	845	845	5	5
Cafe Matthew													
Beef Tenderloin	1/8	840	585	63	27	32	11	311	189	275	350	0	0
Dijon Vinaigrette	1/6	500		55		8		36		125		0	
Chocolate Velvet Cake	1/10	740	500	52	27	29	14	224	1	440	390	2	1
Cilantro & Jalapeño Cream	1/6	590	170	60	1	37	0	224	7	85	215	0	0
Tortilla Soup	1/6	360	180	23	8	7	2	74	12	1230	1050	4	3
Carriage House													
Grilled Mushrooms/Peppers	1/4	235	75	23	5	6	1	15	3	335	150	1	1
Five Onion Soup	1/6	680	295	50	11	28	5	133	19	1825	960	3	2
Salmon/Vinaigrette/Spinach	1/4	900	315	84	17	23	3	95	29	1810	1300	3	3
Mr. Mac's Salad	1/12	430	225	42	21	7	3	35	9	170	55	2	2
Espresso Torte	1/12	580		50		30		240		325		2	

*The analysis of the original recipe is given in columns labeled O, and followed by values for the modified version in columns labeled M.

NUTRITIONAL ANALYSIS*

	Portion of Recipe	Calories		Fat (grams)		Saturated Fat (grams)		Cholesterol (milligrams)		Sodium (milligrams)		Dietary Fiber (grams)	
		O	M	O	M	O	M	O	M	O	M	O	M
Carshon's Delicatessen													
Chicken Soup With Kreplach	1/8	200		6		2		115		915		1	
Reuben Sandwich	1/2	705	450	45	22	20	9	200	105	2910	2095	5	5
Carshon Bars	1/32	340	285	16	10	8	4	36	6	260	180	2	2
Stuffed Cabbage	1/6	325	250	12	2	5	1	51	40	1025	660	3	3
French Coconut Pie	1/16	565	400	35	16	14	4	113	0	425	405	1	1
Joe T. Garcia's													
Huevos Rancheros	1/2	500	325	32	14	6	4	470	430	600	580	5	5
Salsa Ranchera	1/8	25	10	2	0	0	0	0	0	85	85	0	0
Carne Asada	1/6	300	250	18	13	6	5	100	100	155	175	0	0
Migas	1/2	790	415	50	8	9	2	500	75	375	395	6	6
Guacamole	1/4	135		12		2		0		30		3	
Salsa Tomate Verde/Aguacate	1/12	75		5		1		0		220		2	
Sopa de Tortilla	1/6	630	275	45	10	15	3	50	13	1260	1175	8	6
Hedary's & Byblos													
Hummus	1/8	475	300	30	13	4	2	0	0	2050	575	11	11
Kibbi	1/8	250		10		3		74		330		4	
Ablama	1/4	480	245	34	13	9	3	76	36	635	185	6	6
Tabbuli	1/6	170	110	10	3	1	0	0	0	550	195	5	5
Mahshe Warak Aresh	1/4	260	260	10	10	3	3	74	74	2090	760	2	2
Iron Horse Cafe													
Olive Soup	1/5	335	210	29	11	17	2	88	3	1020	1065	1	1
Buttermilk Pie	1/8	380	380	18	17	7	4	98	81	425	430	0	0
Holiday Roast	1/8	840		57		23		158		180		5	
Pecan Pie	1/8	490	470	27	25	7	4	96	0	360	370	1	1
King Ranch Casserole	1/9	330	275	17	10	7	4	67	56	895	620	2	2
Two Minute Fudge	1/32	85		3		2		9		35		0	
Kimbell Museum Buffet													
Wild Mushroom Soup	1/4	450	350	16	3	8	1	43	2	1120	1120	5	5
Orzo Pasta	1/6	195		2		0		0		95		3	
Black Bean Pizza	1/8	365		7		3		11		615		5	
Chocolate Chip Cake	1/12	640	445	32	11	16	3	136	0	350	285	2	2
Texas Lamb Stew	1/12	485	380	30	22	7	6	100	75	640	625	5	5
la Madeleine													
Poulet au Vinaigre	1/8	340	200	23	8	9	2	112	85	250	250	0	0
Flan au Champignons	1/4	290	100	22	1	11	0	362	2	315	335	0	0
Zucchini Flan	1/6	800	180	84	8	51	2	390	3	670	335	1	1
Fruit Taboule	1/6	160		0		0		0		8		1	
Soufflé Citron	1/4	125		6		2		213		70		0	

*The analysis of the original recipe is given in columns labeled O, and followed by values for the modified version in columns labeled M.

NUTRITIONAL ANALYSIS*

	Portion of Recipe	Calories		Fat (grams)		Saturated Fat (grams)		Cholesterol (milligrams)		Sodium (milligrams)		Dietary Fiber (grams)	
		O	M	O	M	O	M	O	M	O	M	O	M
La Piazza													
Misto Mare Piazza	1/4	650	540	23	10	9	2	229	195	660	575	5	5
Lumache Bellavista	1/2	355	330	10	6	4	1	130	114	390	365	1	1
Costata di Vitello	1/2	750	460	41	9	9	4	565	140	1000	1025	2	2
Scaloppine Alla Genovese	1/2	550	270	38	8	16	3	167	97	387	310	2	2
Insalata Di Pesce	1/8	1060	415	86	12	12	2	380	380	600	600	4	4
Le Chardonnay													
African Queen	1/4	960	500	66	5	40	2	230	14	525	495	4	4
Potato Au Gratin Dauphinois	1/4	615	275	53	5	33	3	190	20	435	505	3	3
La Daurade Au Four	1/4	345		9		1		60		365		2	
Vinaigrette de la Maman Tonia	1/4	185	110	16	8	2	1	53	0	360	370	3	3
Pot Au Feu d'Agneau	1/4	1490	700	69	16	21	5	290	99	2150	1200	7	8
Lucile's													
Meat Loaf With Tomato Sauce	1/5	450	380	26	19	9	7	134	85	1010	1000	2	3
Crab Cakes /Garlic Cream	1/5	850	400	72	22	11	3	274	155	1200	875	0	0
Fisherman's Stew	1/4	830	440	42	9	18	2	260	90	2775	2525	6	6
Michaels													
Ranch Goat Cheese Canapes	1/2	55		4		1		5		120		0	
Texas Bobwhite Quail	1/6	275		8		1		50		45		2	
Ranch Pralines	1/48	90		3		1		5		30		0	
Sunset Ranch Margarita	1/6	215		0		0		0		5		0	
NM Cafe													
Chicken Hunter Style	1/8	345	290	14	8	6	2	125	108	390	260	1	1
Duke of Windsor Sandwich	1	450		10		5		65		690		4	
NM Pasta Giovanni	1/6	450	410	19	14	3	3	4	4	195	195	3	3
Popovers	1/24	75	50	3	0	1	0	45	0	70	70	0	0
New Mexico Sandwich	1	700	472	39	18	15	7	120	79	930	535	2	2
Old Swiss House													
Cucumber Soup	1/6	320	150	26	3	15	1	84	3	635	610	2	2
Veal Oscar	1/4	770	390	60	13	35	6	400	175	860	635	3	2
Les Crevettes D'Espagna	1/10	615	300	57	17	34	9	383	170	1255	990	1	1
Filet Wellington	1/10	930	585	57	24	21	9	300	180	1105	740	1	2
On Broadway & Portofino													
Lentil Soup	1/8	230		6		1		33		560		10	
Linguine With White Clam Sauce	1/4	770	425	43	4	6	0	50	50	385	385	3	3
Osso Bucco	1/4	475	420	18	11	3	2	117	117	1230	1230	3	3
Profiteroles	1/6	400	250	28	10	16	4	249	2	170	160	1	1

*The analysis of the original recipe is given in columns labeled O, and followed by values for the modified version in columns labeled M.

NUTRITIONAL ANALYSIS*

	Portion of Recipe	Calories		Fat (grams)		Saturated Fat (grams)		Cholesterol (milligrams)		Sodium (milligrams)		Dietary Fiber (grams)	
		O	M	O	M	O	M	O	M	O	M	O	M
Piccolo Mondo													
Angel Hair Pasta/Sea Scallops	1/5	600	470	23	8	8	1	62	35	690	590	2	2
Mussels Alla Marinara	1/6	350	215	22	7	7	1	80	57	685	605	1	1
Alaskan Salmon/Basil & Cream	1/4	800	315	63	13	37	3	235	41	1870	1450	0	0
Roasted Peppers	1/4	285	105	27	7	4	1	0	0	150	150	4	4
Broiled Veal Chops	1/4	335	225	20	7	11	2	158	115	365	265	1	1
Cream Caramel	1/4	300	235	10	0	4	0	230	4	130	185	0	0
Razzoo's Cajun Cafe													
Chicken Tchoupitoulas	1/4	1070	350	90	10	38	3	410	147	1600	840	1	1
Crawfish Hollandaise	1/8	345	130	37	12	17	2	150	37	475	250	0	0
Grilled 'Gator Tail	1/4	600	360	40	12	22	4	167	85	1135	920	2	2
BBQ "Ouch" Sauce	1/64	175	40	18	2	11	0	47	0	400	280	0	0
Jambalaya	1/10	330	300	13	10	6	3	58	40	690	640	2	2
Roasted Redskin Potaotes	1/6	185	130	9	2	1	0	0	0	405	370	3	3
Reflections													
Vine-Ripe Tomatoes	1/4	570	235	49	15	17	6	76	23	390	250	3	3
Frozen Grand Marnier Soufflé	1/6	450		20		11		269		85		0	
Fillet of Salmon	1/4	1450	410	137	11	82	2	420	33	2105	1270	4	4
Grilled Veal Rib-eye	1/4	710	280	49	8	25	2	264	110	800	185	2	2
Saint-Emilion													
Filet de Boeuf	1/4	785	470	60	24	31	8	235	128	717	361	0	0
Aumoniere Au Crabe	1/12	180	160	9	7	5	4	95	55	200	197	1	1
Steak de Thon au Poivre	1/4	670	400	45	14	24	3	200	83	461	350	1	1
Moules/Pineau des Charentes	1/4	850	315	59	10	33	2	329	86	813	735	0	0

*The analysis of the original recipe is given in columns labeled O, and followed by values for the modified version in columns labeled M.

INDEX

WHO'S WHO

From top left,

1 **Bill Bostelmann,** *Flowers on the Square*
2 **Reinhard Warmuth,** *Cactus Bar & Grill*
3 **Franco Hedary,** *Hedary's*
4 **Kevin Kelly,** *Radisson Hotel*
5 **Michel Baudouin,** *Le Chardonnay*
6 **John Kennedy,** *Michaels*
7 **Michael Thomson,** *Michaels*
8 **Lizzie Lancarte,** *Joe T. Garcia's*
9 **Walter Kaufmann,** *Old Swiss House*
10 **Carlo Crocci,** *Bella Italia West*
11 **Mariz Hedary,** *Hedary's*
12 **Keith Crow,** *Computer Programmer*
13 **Patrick Esquerré,** *la Madeleine*
14 **Betty Robinson,** *Carshon's*
15 **Bernard Tronche,** *Saint-Emilion*
16 **Leila Hedary,** *Hedary's*
17 **Jill Fortney,** *Personal Image Consultant*
18 **Cliff Cline,** *Iron Horse Cafe*
19 **Zurella Lancarte,** *Joe T. Garcia's*
20 **Richard Schafer,** *The Worthington*

From lower left,

21 **DeAnna Koch,** *Assistant to Renie Steves*
22 **Nick Saracino,** *Piccolo Mondo*
23 **Alicia Bradshaw,** *Editorial Assistant*
24 **Jean-Claude Adam,** *Cacharel*
25 **Hans Bergmann,** *Cacharel*
26 **Joe T. Lancarte,** *Joe T. Garcia's*
27 **Jean Louis Barrére,** *Reflections*
28 **Philip Lancarte,** *Joe T. Garcia's*
29 **Cherif Brahmi,** *On Broadway*
30 **Wes Glover,** *NM Cafe*

31 **Renie Steves,** *Author*
32 **Janifer Rose,** *NM Cafe*
33 **Mark Davis,** *Photographer*
34 **Sally Bolick,** *Cafe Matthew*
35 **Mike Leatherwood,** *Razzoo's*
36 **Mary Swift,** *Carshon's*
37 **Scott Marks,** *Razzoo's*
38 **Randy Rogers,** *The Worthington*

39 **Paul Willis,** *Lucile's*
40 **James Morris,** *The Worthington*
41 **Shelby Schafer,** *Kimbell Buffet*

Not pictured,

Gerard Bahon, *Bistro Bagatelle*
Marios Hedary, *Byblos*
Willis McIntosh, *Carriage House*
Vito Ciraci, *La Piazza*

CUISINE CONCEPTS ORDER FORM

Name _____

Address _____

City _____ State _____ ZIP _____

My check or money order is enclosed.

❑ **Fort Worth Is Cooking!**   ❑ **Dallas Is Cooking!**

    $16.95 cover price $15.95 cover price
      1.31 Texas sales tax   1.24 Texas sales tax
      2.00 shipping and handling   2.00 shipping and handling
    $20.26 total per copy   **$19.19 total per copy**

Wholesale orders are welcome! Qualified buyers please contact Cuisine Concepts at 817/732-4758 or fax 817/732-3247 for details.

Make checks payable to:

Cuisine Concepts
1406 Thomas Place
Fort Worth, Texas 76107-2432

CUISINE CONCEPTS ORDER FORM

Name _____

Address _____

City _____ State _____ ZIP _____

My check or money order is enclosed.

❑ **Fort Worth Is Cooking!**   ❑ **Dallas Is Cooking!**

    $16.95 cover price $15.95 cover price
      1.31 Texas sales tax   1.24 Texas sales tax
      2.00 shipping and handling   2.00 shipping and handling
    $20.26 total per copy   **$19.19 total per copy**

Wholesale orders are welcome! Qualified buyers please contact Cuisine Concepts at 817/732-4758 or fax 817/732-3247 for details.

Make checks payable to:

Cuisine Concepts
1406 Thomas Place
Fort Worth, Texas 76107-2432